The THIMBLEBERRIES Guide for Weekend Quilters

The THIMBLEBERRIES
Guide for Weekend Quilters

25 Great-Looking Quilts for the Busy Quiltmaker

LYNETTE JENSEN

Rodale Press, Inc.
Emmaus, Pennsylvania

Editor: **Jane Townswick**

Interior Book Designer: **Nancy Smola Biltcliff**

Layout Designer: **Susan P. Eugster**

Interior Illustrators: **Sandy Freeman, Susan Hunt Yule (page 1, map), and Jane D. Ramsey (pages 3, 4, and 6)**

Cover and Interior Photographer: **Mitch Mandel**

Interior Photo Stylist: **Marianne Grape Laubach**

Cover Designers: **Marta Mitchell Strait (front) and Robin M. Hepler (back)**

Photography Editor: **James A. Gallucci**

Copy Editors: **Ann Snyder and Liz Leone**

Manufacturing Coordinator: **Patrick T. Smith**

Indexer: **Nan N. Badgett**

RODALE HOME AND GARDEN BOOKS

Vice President and Editorial Director: **Margaret J. Lydic**

Managing Editor, Rodale Quilt Books: **Suzanne Nelson**

Director of Design and Production: **Michael Ward**

Associate Art Director: **Carol Angstadt**

Production Manager: **Robert V. Anderson Jr.**

Studio Manager: **Leslie M. Keefe**

Copy Director: **Dolores Plikaitis**

Manufacturing Manager: **Mark Krahforst**

Office Manager: **Karen Earl-Braymer**

ON THE COVER:
Quilts in top row, left to right:
Starburst Table Runner, Piece of Cake, Independence
Quilts in middle row, left to right:
Picnic Table Runner, Climbing Vines, Fall Colors
Quilts in bottom row, left to right:
Thimbleberries Mix, Welcome Home, My Stars

Library of Congress Cataloging-in-Publication Data

Jensen, Lynette.
The Thimbleberries guide for weekend quilters : 25 great-looking projects for the busy quiltmaker / Lynette Jensen.
p. cm.
Includes index.
ISBN 0–87596–812–0 hardcover
1. Patchwork—Patterns. 2. Quilting—Patterns.
I. Thimbleberries, Inc. II. Title.
TT835.J47 1999
746.46'041—dc21

98–51229

2 4 6 8 10 9 7 5 3 hardcover

To Suzanne and her team

C·O·N·T·E·N·T·S

A·C·K·N·O·W·L·E·D·G·M·E·N·T·S

As Thimbleberries, Inc., has grown over the last 10 years, I've become more and more aware of my good fortune in being surrounded by an extraordinary group of talented and energetic people who help turn my designs into the patterns, books, and fabrics that have been embraced by so many quiltmakers. It has been a great blessing to work with the same dedicated staff in my studio over the years, as well as the stitchers and quilters whose efforts make my quilt designs spring to life—

my heartfelt thanks to Sue Bahr, Julie Borg, Peggy Christianson, Esther Grischkowsky, Sherry Husske, Julie Jergens, Lisa Kirchoff, Kathy Lobeck, Carla Plowman, Leone Rusch, and Tracy Schrantz.

Thanks, too, to all of the quilters who contributed many wonderful tips and information featured in the "Weekend Quilter Profiles"—Kathie Haddock, Lisa Kirchoff, Sandy Lavin, Suzanne Nelson, Susie Lenz, Jamie O'Brien, and Joanne Wilson.

Throughout all three of my books, I have had the pleasure of working with Suzanne Nelson, the quilt book editors at Rodale Press, and a wonderful team of designers, photographers, and illustrators. We have become friends with a common goal—to produce the best quilt books ever. Thank you all for helping showcase my designs that enable quilters to make beautiful quilts.

I·N·T·R·O·D·U·C·T·I·O·N

Thimbleberries quilts are known for their signature style, color combinations, and, most importantly, the ease of construction that is an important feature of all of my designs. As my involvement in the world of quiltmaking has expanded, I've enjoyed traveling and meeting many wonderful people who have truly embraced my style of quiltmaking. It is heartwarming to hear comments that echo what I have always known—simply put, that quilters love color, fabric, sewing, and making quilts for their homes, families, and friends. We are busy people who find ways to fit our hobby into the few, precious hours between jobs, family, and community responsibilities.

In designing the wide variety of quilts in the pages that follow, I've kept three important things in mind—good looks, time, and ease of construction. I'm always amazed at the dramatic impact that fabric can have on a room, and I think you will enjoy the warmth and charm that the Thimbleberries palette will bring to your quilts. You'll also be pleasantly surprised at how quick and easy it is to assemble each project, with simple, straightforward instructions and slightly oversize pieces. You'll find full-size bed quilts that will add warmth and charm to any room—many of which can be pieced in a weekend. Many of the wall quilts and table runners and the tree skirt make great gifts and room brighteners. And finally, 18 of the quilts feature "House Dressing" companion projects— fast and fabulous accessories that will help you put your personal touch on any room in your home. I hope you will enjoy making these quilts and using them to add beauty to your life.

Lynette Jensen

Lynette Jensen

BUSY QUILTER'S SURVIVAL GUIDE

Over the years I've met hundreds of quilters who tell me the same thing —I wish I had more time to quilt. I've also noticed how people who love quilting always manage to find a way to make it fit into a busy life. They don't let a crowded schedule cut them off completely from their quilting. When free time gets scarce, they get creative in carving out time for the craft they love. Busy women, more than anyone else, really need and deserve a little "fabric therapy." In this section I've collected real-life strategies from quilters who have found ways to make sure that quilting is a regular part of their life, both on weekdays and weekends.

TIME MAKERS

No matter how hard we try to stretch them, there are still always going to be only 24 hours in a day. The trick is how to claim chunks of time and turn them into opportunities to stitch.

Finding "Lost" Time

Don't let these common time bandits rob you of valuable chances to work on your quilts.

Phone Time

Cellular and portable telephones make it easy to continue with tasks like machine piecing, machine quilting, pressing, and any kind of hand work while you chat. Consider treating yourself to a shoulder rest for the phone, so you can avoid neck or back strain while sewing. If you don't have a portable phone, look into a headset attachment that will allow you to stitch and talk at the same time in comfort. The only important warning: Don't try to talk and rotary cut at the same time. Working with that sharp tool in your hand demands total concentration.

TV Time

Never sit empty handed. Save hand work like quilting, appliqué, stitching down binding, or attaching labels and hanging sleeves for evenings when you know you'll be in front of the TV. Practice the quilter's trick of "listening" to a television program or video. You'll learn to look up to catch the good parts. To make the most of this time, keep a separate TV set of tools on a table next to your favorite chair. When you have a second set of things like scissors, threads, pins, and needles always ready, you won't waste time chasing them down. A lidded wooden or fabric-covered basket keeps things neat and tidy in between sewing sessions.

Kitchen Duty

Capture those snippets of down time while you're in the kitchen. While you're waiting for the pasta water to boil, consider tracing some appliqué shapes onto pieces of freezer paper. While the cookies are baking, trim the dog ears off a batch of triangle squares. Trace and cut out several appliqué shapes. Pin binding in place. Any project task that involves only one or two supplies is one that you can bring into the kitchen and do easily at the counter or kitchen table. Because you'll want to be able to set up and clear away quickly, use a small plastic storage bin to hold the bits and pieces of these time-filler projects. If your sewing room is located near the kitchen and it's easy to dart back and forth, set your kitchen timer as a reminder to check on what's cooking.

Sleep

Knowing that many people feel like they don't get quite enough, it's tricky business calling sleep a "time bandit." After all, your health and well-being depend on getting enough rest. But consider this: Getting up just half an hour earlier one day a week gives you 26 extra hours a year to quilt. Make that three days of early rising and you gain 78 more hours. Five days a week yields a bonus 130 hours. You can do a lot of quiltmaking with any of those extra pockets of time. The quiet, uninterrupted period before the rest of the family gets up could be some of the most productive time you spend, not to mention a blissful way to start the day.

Take Control of the Calendar

Fitting activities into a busy schedule relies on one very simple principle—to make time for something that's important to you, block it out on the calendar and stick to it.

The 15-Minute Commitment

Make a promise to yourself that you'll spend at least 15 minutes every night stitching. No matter how many other things fill your evening, finding 15 minutes is manageable. It may not sound like much, but you'll be surprised at how far you can get by working in small increments of time.

Designate Official Quilting Time

Schedule a certain portion of each day or each week as "my quilting time" on your family calendar. Let your husband, children, and friends know you're serious about not being interrupted. Let them answer the phone and the doorbell. Tell them you'll return messages when you're done. The next, most important part of this— don't feel guilty about doing something that is satisfying to your soul.

Group Support System

This is where having quilting friends comes in handy. Pick one day a week or month and designate that as your sewing day, when you get together and quilt. Write this in ink on your calendar. Take turns gathering at each other's house, bring lunches so there's no burden on the hostess, and work on your own or joint projects. The point is that you've committed to this time with friends so it's harder to get distracted and let other things take over the time.

Attitude Adjustments

Making time for quilting sometimes means overcoming nagging feelings about housekeeping chores not attended to or time spent apart from spouse and children. Here are a couple ways to relieve any vestige of quilt guilt.

Lower Your Housekeeping Expectations

What gives you more satisfaction—dusting the mini-blinds or piecing a quilt top? Which do you think your family will appreciate most? Which handiwork will your neighbors admire? There's a lot of wisdom in the bumper sticker that reads: Quilting forever, housework whenever. Clutter is not life-threatening. When you have a free half hour, ignore the voice in your head that says "finish the dishes….fold the laundry." Spend that time working on a quilt that will add beauty and joy to your life.

Bring Your Family into the Fold

There will be fewer interruptions and complaints about time spent in your sewing room when you recruit your family to join you. Young children can mark templates. Older siblings can draw appliqué shapes onto fusible webbing and learn to wield a rotary cutter, and a husband can be a great help in layering a finished quilt or putting a project into a floor frame. When your family is involved, they'll be more enthusiastic about and appreciate your passion for making quilts. Plus, you'll plant some seeds for the next generation of quilters.

PLAN AHEAD

Here's the secret to fitting quiltmaking into a busy life: Divide and conquer. Instead of being overwhelmed by the thought of all the time it takes to make a bed-size quilt, break the project down into smaller tasks and then fit those into the pockets of available time you find scattered throughout the day. Have the supplies ready and waiting so you can jump right in whenever you get the chance. The key is planning ahead and being organized. Look for the clock-face symbol to find tips that will give you specific ideas on how to work in efficient stages. The tips that follow here can be used with any project.

Smart Strategies

Try out these tactics that work well for other busy quilters.

Work in Batches

Concentrating on the same kind of task at one time is more efficient than bouncing back and forth between the sewing machine, ironing board, and cutting mat. Think about how you can group similar tasks over the course of making your quilt. Do all the rotary cutting for the entire quilt in one session. Piece all the triangle squares or strip sets for the quilt in a batch. If there are different sizes, keep them in separate plastic bags labeled by size. Move them over to your ironing board. Wait until you have another window of time, then press them. Move them over to your sewing machine. Whenever you have a few minutes, stitch a few units together. Put them in a pile to be pressed. When you have a sizable group, press them all at once. Batching similar tasks together allows you to make significant headway even when you only have 10 minutes at a time to work.

Organize Your Sewing Space

Keeping your sewing area well stocked and clutter-free is one of the best ways to make your quilting time more efficient.

Post a Supply List

Post a sheet of paper where it is easily visible in your sewing room. Whenever you start to run low on something, add it to your list. You'll be able to plan more efficient shopping trips—and make sure you won't forget something essential.

Use Stackable Storage Systems

Look for clear plastic boxes for storing fabrics and other quilt-making supplies, so you can see everything at a glance. The stackable, drawer-type boxes will help keep everything in your sewing area easily accessible. And try out the array of storage trays from Rubbermaid. The long, narrow trays are great for storing rotary rulers sideways, and the kitchen flatware trays are wonderful for keeping smaller equipment within easy reach of your sewing machine.

Sewing machine needles
Gray thread
Fusible web

Survey Your Stash

Invest a little up-front time to make an inventory of your fabric collection and you'll be able to plan and shop for your quilts much more efficiently. Clip a 1-inch swatch from every piece of fabric and glue each swatch onto its own 3 × 5 index card. (Ask your children or spouse if they'd like to help out with this inventory.) Write down how much of

each fabric you have, where you bought it, who the manufacturer is. Put the cards into a file box. When you want to check on whether you have the perfect green, you can flip through the box quickly, rather than dig through stacks of fabrics. Whenever you want to purchase coordinating fabrics, you'll be able to take your boxed "stash" to the quilt shop.

ROAD TRIPS

Just because you leave the sewing room doesn't mean you have to leave your sewing behind. For busy quilters on the go, here are some tips on how to make the most of the time you spend away from home. The trick is to make your projects and sewing equipment portable.

Travel Accessories for Quilters

✦ **Carry-All:** The Lands' End Original Attaché Case makes a great travel sewing bag. This lightweight, inexpensive bag zips open to lie completely flat. Large enough to easily hold a project, a rotary cutter, a 6 × 12-inch rotary ruler, and a small cutting mat, it will also accommodate other useful supplies and equipment, like pads of paper, quilting books, magazines, graph paper, patterns, scissors, needles, threads, and more.

✦ **Sewing Case:** If you don't want to carry a separate tote bag, look for a small sewing case that you will be able to tuck into your purse comfortably. It should have small compartments that are just large enough to hold spools of thread, needles, embroidery scissors, a thimble, and pins. Keep it filled and ready to go whenever you are.

✦ **Ott-Lite:** This portable electric light is a godsend for anyone who has ever stitched in the substandard lighting of a hotel room. The built-in handle makes it easy to carry, and it folds up to a flat, compact size. Take along an extension cord for times when you're in a large classroom, and you'll always have plenty of light.

✦ **Threaded Needles:** Thread a dozen quilting needles onto a spool of quilting thread before you leave home. This spares you the ordeal of trying to thread the eye of a small needle in a moving car, bus, or plane.

✦ **Eyeglass Case:** Recycle an old eyeglass case (the kind that snaps shut) to safely carry a rotary cutter or a pair of scissors.

✦ **Daisy Pins:** Use these extra-long pins with the daisy-head as an anchor to hold spools or scissors when you're stitching on a bus or plane. Stick the pin into the seat in front of you. Slide the spool or scissors handle over the pin and you won't have to worry about chasing them down.

✦ **Self-Sealing Plastic Bags:** Hand-sewing projects are obviously the most portable. Appliqué, buttonhole stitching, bindings, and yo-yos are some quilting jobs that are easy to do on the go. Put your project in a plastic bag that seals along the top and you won't have to worry about losing bits and pieces. Pop in a small pair of scissors, thread, needles, and pins and you'll have everything you need in one place.

MAKE IT TONIGHT OR MAKE IT IN A WEEKEND

Keep your eyes open for the "Make It Tonight" or "Make It in a Weekend" icons appearing with many of the projects in this book. These icons indicate quilts that are particularly quick and easy to make. While we were making the sample quilts shown in the photographs, we kept track of the amount of time it took for each. We didn't race the clock—we put them together at a pace that is pretty typical of a quiltmaker sewing at home. The ones that can be easily assembled in 3 to 4 hours earned the "Make It Tonight" designation. Projects that can tend to take a bit more time—anywhere from 6 to 12 hours—carry the "Make It in a Weekend" label.

Turn to the contents page for the easiest way to see at a glance which quilts in the book carry these special time ratings, and you'll be able to select projects that are just right for your available time.

MAKE IT TONIGHT

MAKE IT IN A WEEKEND

SEW EASY, SEW FAST QUILTS

Quilts add beauty to our lives in many ways. In our home surroundings, they reveal our personal color and style preferences. As seasons of the year go by, the things we see in nature often come out in our choices of colors and fabrics we put into quilts—warm shades of summer; deep, crisp colors of autumn; the sharp contrasts of lights and darks in winter; and lighter, brighter palettes when spring emerges again. Whatever ways you love to use quilts in your life, whether for seasonal or holiday decorating, celebrating special occasions, making gifts for people you love, or simply indulging your passion for creativity and self-expression, you'll find quilts in this section that are fast and fun to make, with large, easy-to-cut pieces that will produce spectacular results.

PIECE OF CAKE

SIZE

Bed Quilt: 80 × 104 inches (unquilted)
Finished Block: 8 inches square

 ## HOUSE DRESSING

See the Button-Trimmed Pillowcases on the bed.
Directions are given on page 15.

FABRICS AND SUPPLIES

Yardage is based on 44-inch-wide fabric.

- ✦ 2⅜ yards chestnut print fabric for Checkerboard Strips and Triangle Blocks
- ✦ 2⅜ yards blue print fabric for Checkerboard Strips and Triangle Blocks
- ✦ 2⅜ yards beige print fabric for Triangle Blocks
- ✦ 2¾ yards blue plaid #1 fabric for border
- ✦ 1 yard blue plaid #2 fabric for bias binding
- ✦ 7½ yards fabric for quilt backing
- ✦ Quilt batting, at least 84 × 108 inches
- ✦ Rotary cutter, mat, and wide see-through ruler with ⅛-inch markings

Color Play

See page 12 for a creative color variation
on the quilt shown here.

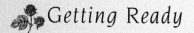 ## Getting Ready

❧ Read instructions thoroughly before you begin.

❧ Prewash and press fabric.

❧ Place right sides of fabric pieces together, and use ¼-inch seam allowances throughout unless directions specify otherwise.

❧ Seam allowances are included in the cutting sizes given.

❧ Press seam allowances in the direction that will create the least bulk, and whenever possible, press toward the darker fabric. Press border seam allowances toward the borders unless directions specify otherwise.

❧ Cutting directions for each section of the quilt are given individually. If you like to cut as you go, simply follow the directions as you get to them. If you'd rather cut all your pieces at the same time, skip ahead to find each of the cutting sections and do all the cutting before you begin.

FABRIC KEY
(for the quilt shown on page 11)

■ Chestnut	■ Blue print	☐ Beige	▦ Blue plaid #1

Color Play

To create an interesting color variation of the quilt on page 11, substitute green for blue, and use lighter beiges and reds rather than the beige and chestnut prints. I decided on a large-scale floral border print to tie all of the colors together, and the effect is a more feminine look than the blue plaid border.

CHECKERBOARD STRIPS

(Make 2)

Cutting

From the chestnut print fabric:
✦ Cut five 6½ × 44-inch strips

From the blue print fabric:
✦ Cut five 6½ × 44-inch strips

Piecing

1 Sew the chestnut and blue 6½-inch-wide strips together in pairs, as shown in **Diagram 1,** and press. Make five strip sets, and cross cut them into twenty-two 8½-inch segments, as shown.

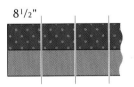

Diagram 1

2 Sew 11 segments together for each Checkerboard Strip, alternating colors, as shown in **Diagram 2.** Make two of these Checkerboard Strips, and press.

Diagram 2

TRIANGLE BLOCKS

(Make 28 blue and beige)

(Make 31 chestnut and beige)

Cutting

From the chestnut print fabric:
✦ Cut four 9¼ × 44-inch strips. From these strips, cut sixteen 9¼-inch squares. Cut the squares diagonally into quarters, forming 64 triangles. You will be using 62 of these triangles.

From the blue print fabric:
✦ Cut four 9¼ × 44-inch strips. From these strips, cut fourteen 9¼-inch squares. Cut the squares diagonally into quarters, forming 56 triangles.

From the beige print fabric:
✦ Cut eight 9¼ × 44-inch strips. From these strips, cut thirty 9¼-inch squares. Cut the squares diagonally into quarters, forming 120 triangles. You will be using 118 of these triangles.

Piecing

1 Layer a blue triangle on a beige triangle, as shown in **Diagram 3.** Stitch along one of the bias edges, being careful not to stretch the triangles, and press. Repeat for the remaining blue and beige triangles. Make sure you sew with the blue fabric on top, and sew along the same bias edge of each triangle set, so that your pieced triangle units will all have the blue triangles on the same side.

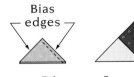

Diagram 3

2 Sew the Step 1 triangle units together in pairs to make the triangle blocks, as shown in **Diagram 4,** and press. Make a total of 28 of these Triangle Blocks. At this point, the Triangle Blocks should measure 8½ inches square.

Diagram 4

3 Layer a chestnut triangle on a beige triangle, as shown in **Diagram 5.** Stitch along one of the bias edges, and press. Repeat for the remaining chestnut and beige triangles. Make sure you sew with the chestnut fabric on top, and sew along the same bias edge of each triangle set so that your pieced triangle units will have the chestnut triangles on the same side.

Diagram 5

4 Sew the Step 3 triangle units together in pairs to make the Triangle Blocks, as shown in **Diagram 6,** and press. Make a total of 31 of these Triangle Blocks. At this point, the Triangle Blocks should measure 8½ inches square.

Diagram 6

QUILT CENTER

1 Sew the Triangle Blocks together, alternating the colors, to form five vertical rows, referring to the **Quilt Diagram** for block placement. Three of the five rows start and end with blue blocks. Two rows start and end with chestnut blocks. The four extra chestnut blocks will be used for the corner squares in the border.

2 Referring to the **Quilt Diagram,** sew the five vertical rows of Triangle Blocks and the two Checkerboard Strips together, and press.

BORDER

The yardage given allows for border pieces to be cut lengthwise. The border strips are longer than necessary and will be trimmed later.

Cutting

From the blue plaid #1 fabric:
✦ Cut two 8½ × 68-inch strips
✦ Cut two 8½ × 92-inch strips

Attaching the Border

1 To attach the 8½-inch-wide blue plaid #1 top and bottom border strips, as shown in the **Quilt Diagram,** refer to page 198 for "Border Instructions."

2 To attach the 8½-inch-wide blue plaid #1 side border strips with Triangle Block corner squares, as shown in the **Quilt Diagram,** refer to page 200 for "Borders with Corner Squares."

PUTTING IT ALL TOGETHER

1 Cut the 7½-yard length of backing fabric in thirds crosswise to make three 2½-yard lengths. Remove the selvages and sew the long edges together. Press the seam allowances open. Trim the backing and batting so they are about 4 inches larger than the quilt top.

2 For quilting ideas, see the **Quilting Design Diagram.** See page 201 for detailed marking, layering, and finishing instructions.

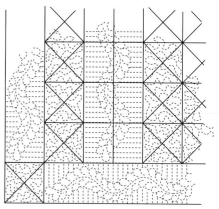

Quilting Design Diagram

BINDING

The 2¾-inch binding strips will produce a ½-inch-wide finished binding. If you want a wider or narrower binding, adjust the width of the strips you cut. (See page 201 for pointers on how to experiment with binding width.) Refer to "Attaching Binding with Mitered Corners" on page 202 to complete your quilt.

Cutting Bias Strips

From the blue plaid #2 binding fabric:
✦ Cut enough 2¾-inch-wide bias strips to make a 390-inch-long strip

Quilt Diagram

Button-Trimmed Pillowcases

1 Measure the entire distance around the middle of your pillow, and add 1 inch to allow for a ½-inch side seam allowance. Measure the length of your pillow, and add 1 inch to allow for a ½-inch seam allowance at each end of the pillow sham. Cut your pillow sham fabric to these measurements.

2 For contrasting trim, cut a 13-inch-wide piece of fabric the same length as the first measurement from Step 1, including the ½-inch seam allowance. With wrong sides together, fold the trim in half lengthwise, and press.

3 Pin the folded trim to the wrong side of the pillow sham fabric and stitch, using a ½-inch seam allowance, as shown in **Diagram 1.**

NOTE: *Additional piping or lace trim can be added at this time. Edge stitch the folded trim in place, as in Step 4.*

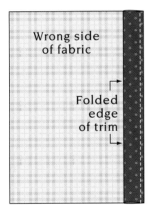

Diagram 1

4 Fold the trim to the right side of the pillow, so that the folded edge of the trim just covers the stitching line, and edge stitch.

5 With right sides together, stitch the end and side of the pillow sham, as shown in **Diagram 2,** using a ½-inch seam allowance. Turn the pillow sham right side out.

Diagram 2

6 Add several buttons, evenly spaced and centered along the trim, as shown in **Diagram 3.** Use fewer buttons if they are large, and more if you use smaller ones. This is a wonderful spot to feature interesting antique buttons or some of the fun, new handmade buttons now available. Make buttonholes for easy removal of the pillow. If your pillow will be purely decorative, this may not be necessary.

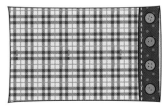

Diagram 3

CHRISTMAS GOOSE

SIZE

Wall Quilt: 66 × 75 inches (unquilted)
Finished Block: 3 × 6 inches

HOUSE DRESSING

See the Curtain with Prairie Points at the window.
Directions are given on page 21.

FABRICS AND SUPPLIES

Yardage is based on 44-inch-wide fabric. For ⅛-yard pieces of fabric, approximately half of each piece will be left over for another project.

- ✦ ½ yard each of 5 beige print fabrics (or assorted fabrics to total 2½ yards) for Flying Geese Blocks

- ✦ ⅛ yard each of 40 dark print fabrics (or assorted fabrics to total 2½ yards) for Flying Geese Blocks

- ✦ 2½ yards red print fabric for vertical lattice strips and outer border

- ✦ ⅜ yard brown print fabric for inner border

- ✦ ¾ yard red print fabric for binding

- ✦ 4 yards fabric for quilt backing

- ✦ Quilt batting, at least 70 × 80 inches

- ✦ Rotary cutter, mat, and wide see-through ruler with ⅛-inch markings

Color Play

See page 18 for a creative color variation
on the quilt shown here.

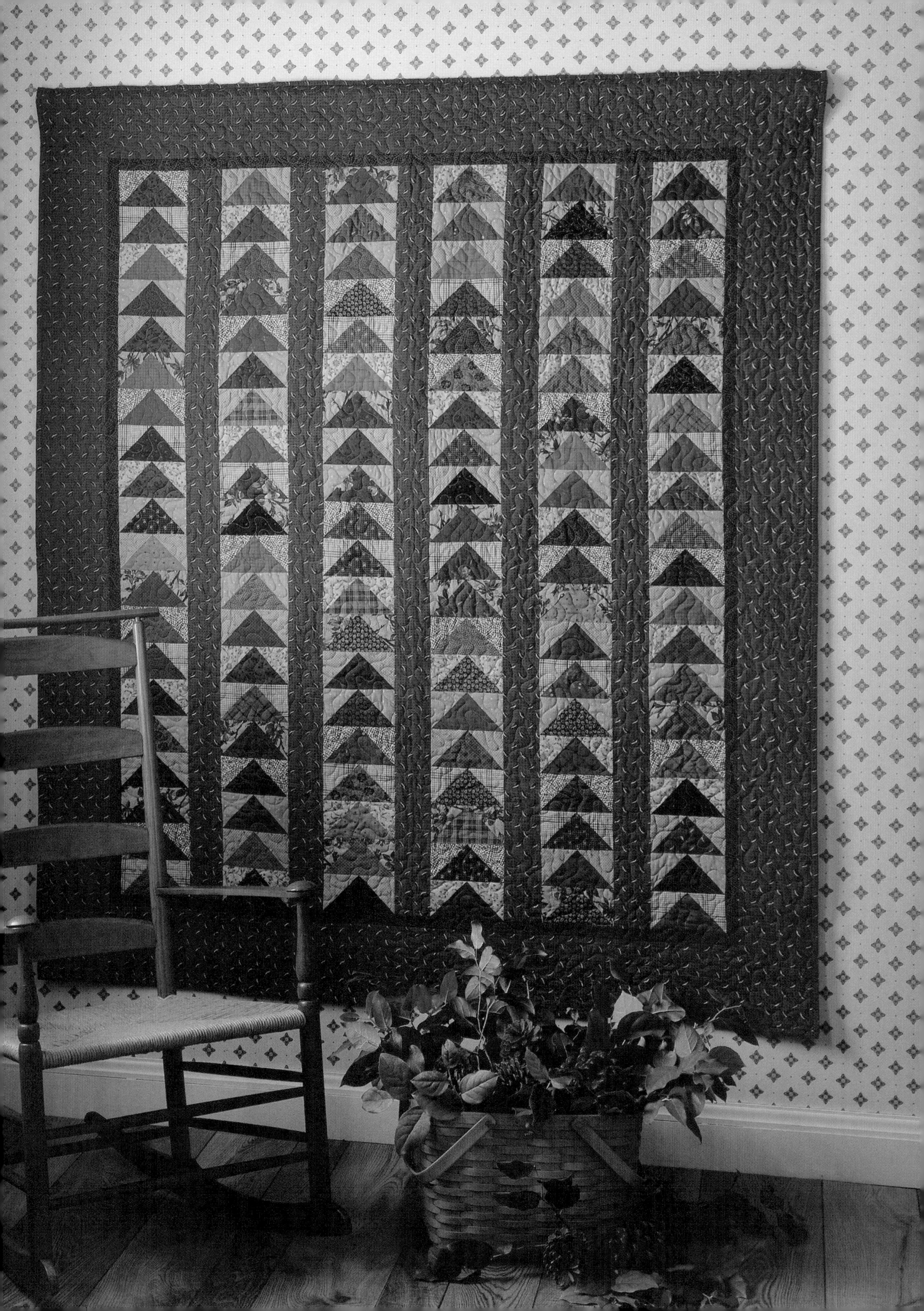

Getting Ready

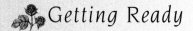

- Read instructions thoroughly before you begin.

- Prewash and press fabric.

- Place right sides of fabric pieces together and use ¼-inch seam allowances throughout unless directions specify otherwise.

- Seam allowances are included in the cutting sizes given.

- Press seam allowances in the direction that will create the least bulk, and whenever possible, press toward the darker fabric. Press border seam allowances toward the borders unless directions specify otherwise.

- Cutting directions for each section of the quilt are given individually. If you like to cut as you go, simply follow the directions as you get to them. If you'd rather cut all your pieces at the same time, skip ahead to find each of the cutting sections and do all the cutting before you begin.

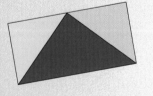

FABRIC KEY
(for the quilt shown on page 17)

Color Play

Darker color values in the "geese" triangles create a rich color variation on the Christmas Goose quilt on page 17. I chose subdued shades of beige and a deeper red print in the border to complete this subtle color scheme.

FLYING GEESE BLOCKS

(Make 120)

Cutting

From the beige print fabrics:
✦ Cut a total of two hundred forty 3½-inch squares

From each of the 40 dark print fabrics:
✦ Cut three 3½ × 6½-inch rectangles, for a total of 120

Piecing

1 Position a 3½-inch beige square on the corner of each 3½ × 6½-inch dark rectangle, as shown at the top of **Diagram 1.** Stitch diagonally from corner to corner on the beige square, as shown. Trim the seam allowance to ¼ inch, and press. Repeat at the opposite corner of the dark rectangles to make the Flying Geese Block, as shown at the bottom of the diagram, and press. Make a total of 120 Flying Geese Blocks. At this point, the Flying Geese Blocks should measure 3½ × 6½ inches.

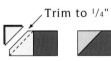
Trim to ¼"

Trim to ¼"

Diagram 1

2 Referring to the **Quilt Diagram** on page 20, sew the Flying Geese Blocks together in six vertical rows of 20 blocks each. Press the seam allowances toward the dark fabric.

3 Measure each vertical row of Flying Geese Blocks. At this point, each row should measure 3½ × 60½ inches. Adjust the seam allowances if the rows are not the same length.

QUILT CENTER

Cutting

From the red print fabric:
✦ Cut ten 3½ × 44-inch strips

Assembly

1 Diagonally piece the ten 3½ × 44-inch red strips together. Cut five 3½-inch-wide red strips to the measurement taken in Step 3, above, for the Flying Geese rows.

2 Referring to the **Quilt Diagram** on page 20, pin and sew the red vertical lattice strips and the Flying Geese rows together. Press the seam allowances toward the red lattice strips.

To make the piecing process for Christmas Goose more efficient, plan on chain piecing all of the left-hand triangles at one time, rather than completing each Flying Geese Block individually. Then do the same with the right-hand triangles.

BORDERS

The yardage given allows for the border strips to be cut on the crosswise grain. The border strips are longer than necessary and will be trimmed later.

Cutting

From the brown print fabric:
✦ Cut six 1½ × 44-inch strips for the inner border

From the red print fabric:
✦ Cut seven 6½ × 44-inch strips for the outer border

Attaching the Borders

1 To attach the 1½-inch-wide brown inner border strips, as shown in the **Quilt Diagram** on page 20, refer to page 198 for "Border Instructions."

When traveling to quilt classes where you will be using your sewing machine, fill up several bobbins ahead of time with medium-toned, neutral threads that will blend in with an array of colorful fabrics like the ones used in Christmas Goose. You'll be able to piece almost any combination of colors together easily, and you can use different top and bobbin colors—like a medium taupe thread on top and a chestnut shade in the bobbin—as long as they are neutrals.

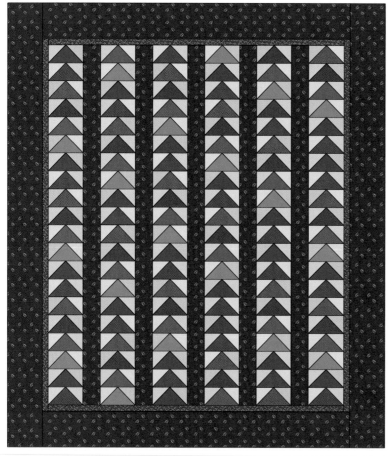

Quilt Diagram

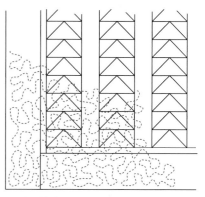

Quilting Design Diagram

2 For quilting ideas, see the **Quilting Design Diagram.** See page 201 for detailed marking, layering, and finishing instructions.

BINDING

The 2¾-inch binding strips will produce a ½-inch-wide finished binding. If you want a wider or narrower binding, adjust the width of the strips you cut. (See page 201 for pointers on how to experiment with binding width.) Refer to "Attaching Binding with Mitered Corners" on page 202 to complete your quilt.

Cutting Crosswise Strips

From the red print binding fabric:
✦ Cut eight 2¾ × 44-inch strips on the crosswise grain

2 To attach the 6½-inch-wide red outer border strips, as shown in the **Quilt Diagram,** refer to "Border Instructions" on page 198.

PUTTING IT ALL TOGETHER

1 Cut the 4-yard length of backing in half crosswise to make two 2-yard lengths. Remove the selvages and sew the long edges together. Press the seam allowances open. Trim the backing and batting so they are about 4 inches larger than the quilt top.

HOUSE DRESSING

Curtain with Prairie Points

Cutting

1 For the curtain, measure the width of your window. Multiply this number by 2, and add 4 inches to allow for side hems. For the upper curtain section, cut one strip of fabric 18 inches wide by this distance. For the lower curtain section, cut one strip 5½ inches wide by the same distance.

2 For the prairie points, measure your window width, and multiply this number by 2. You will need three 5½-inch squares for every 15-inch length of curtain.

Prairie Points

1 Fold a 5½-inch square in half diagonally, as shown in **Diagram 1,** and press. Fold it in half again, as shown, and press.

Fold line

Fold

Fold

Raw edges

Diagram 1

2 Repeat Step 1 to make as many prairie points as necessary for your curtain.

Lower Curtain Trim Section

1 To hem the curtain trim section, turn the bottom edge under 1 inch and press. Turn under another inch, and stitch.

2 Pin and baste the prairie points in place along the raw edge, starting and ending 2 inches in from the sides, as shown in **Diagram 2,** and overlapping them about ⅞ inch. If necessary, you can make small adjustments to space the prairie points evenly over the entire length of the curtain,

rather than making adjustments in only one or two places.

1" hem

Diagram 2

Upper Curtain Section

1 Using a ½-inch seam allowance, sew the 18-inch-wide upper curtain section to the top of the curtain trim section, referring to **Diagram 3.** Fold the sides under 1 inch, and press. Turn under another inch, and stitch the hem, as shown.

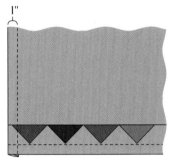

1"

Diagram 3

2 Turn the top raw edge under 4½ inches, and press. Turn it under another 4½ inches and press, as shown in **Diagram 4.** Sew 3 inches in from the top fold to form the header ruffle. Stitch 1½ inches in from the previous stitching to make the rod casing.

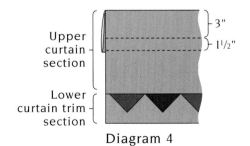

Upper curtain section

3"

1½"

Lower curtain trim section

Diagram 4

FALL COLORS

SIZE

Bed Quilt: 84 × 108 inches (unquilted)
Finished Blocks: 12 inches square

 ## HOUSE DRESSING

See the Fabric-Trimmed Rug on the floor beside the bed.
Directions are given on page 28.

FABRICS AND SUPPLIES

Yardage is based on 44-inch-wide fabric.

+ 1¾ yards green print fabric for Leaf Block A and inner border

+ 4 yards red floral fabric for Leaf Block B and middle and outer borders

+ 1⅔ yards beige print fabric for leaf background

+ 1 yard gold print fabric for Square Block C and corner squares

+ 2 yards red print fabric for Square Block C

+ 1 yard green print fabric for binding

+ 7½ yards fabric for quilt backing

+ Quilt batting, at least 88 × 112 inches

+ Rotary cutter, mat, and wide see-through ruler with ⅛-inch markings

Color Play

See page 24 for a creative color variation
on the quilt shown here.

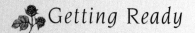
Getting Ready

- Read instructions thoroughly before you begin.

- Prewash and press fabric.

- Place right sides of fabric pieces together, and use ¼-inch seam allowances throughout unless directions specify otherwise.

- Seam allowances are included in the cutting sizes given.

- Press seam allowances in the direction that will create the least bulk, and whenever possible, press toward the darker fabric. Press border seam allowances toward the borders unless directions specify otherwise.

- Cutting directions for each section of the quilt are given individually. If you like to cut as you go, simply follow the directions as you get to them. If you'd rather cut all your pieces at the same time, skip ahead to find each of the cutting sections and do all the cutting before you begin.

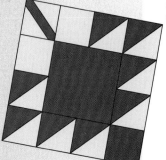

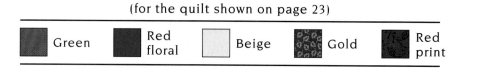

| Green | Red floral | Beige | Gold | Red print |

Color Play

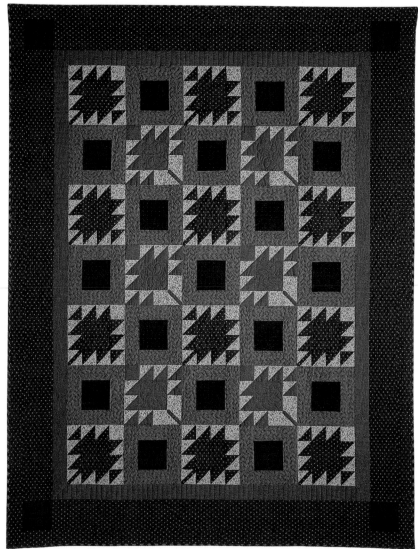

For a creative twist on the Fall Colors quilt shown on page 23, I chose this palette of warm shades, ranging from burnt orange and pumpkin to soft tan, deep brown, and black. The deepness of these colors gives this quilt a warm, cozy look.

LEAF BLOCK A

(Make 6)

LEAF BLOCK B

(Make 12)

Cutting (Leaf Block A)

From the green print fabric:

◆ Cut one $6\frac{1}{2}$ × 44-inch strip. From this strip, cut six $6\frac{1}{2}$-inch squares.

◆ Cut one $3\frac{1}{2}$ × 44-inch strip. From this strip, cut six $3\frac{1}{2}$-inch squares.

◆ Cut three $3\frac{7}{8}$ × 44-inch strips

◆ Cut one $1\frac{1}{4}$ × 44-inch strip. From this strip, cut six $1\frac{1}{4}$ × 6-inch strips.

Cutting (Leaf Block B)

From the red floral fabric:

◆ Cut two $6\frac{1}{2}$ × 44-inch strips. From these strips, cut twelve $6\frac{1}{2}$-inch squares.

◆ Cut six $3\frac{7}{8}$ × 44-inch strips

◆ Cut two $1\frac{1}{4}$ × 44-inch strips. From these strips, cut twelve $1\frac{1}{4}$ × 6-inch strips.

Cutting (Both Leaf Blocks A and B)

From the beige print fabric:

◆ Cut two $3\frac{1}{2}$ × 44-inch strips. From these strips, cut twenty-four $3\frac{1}{2}$-inch squares.

◆ Cut nine $3\frac{7}{8}$ × 44-inch strips

◆ Cut two more $3\frac{1}{2}$ × 44-inch strips. From these strips, cut eighteen $3\frac{1}{2}$-inch squares. Cut these squares in half diagonally.

Piecing Leaf Blocks A and B

1 For Leaf Block A, layer three $3\frac{7}{8}$ × 44-inch green and three $3\frac{7}{8}$ × 44-inch beige strips in pairs, as shown in **Diagram 1,** and press. Cut the layered strips into twenty-four $3\frac{7}{8}$-inch squares, as shown, taking care not to shift the layers as you cut.

Diagram 1

2 Cut the squares in half diagonally, as shown in **Diagram 2.** Stitch $\frac{1}{4}$ inch from the diagonal edges, and press. Make a total of 48 of these triangle-pieced squares. At this point, the triangle-pieced squares should measure $3\frac{1}{2}$ inches square.

Diagram 2

3 For Leaf Block B, repeat Steps 1 and 2, using six $3\frac{7}{8}$ × 44-inch red floral and six $3\frac{7}{8}$ × 44-inch beige strips. Cut the layered strips into sixty $3\frac{7}{8}$-inch squares. Cut these squares in half diagonally, as shown in **Diagram 3.** Stitch $\frac{1}{4}$ inch from the diagonal edges, and press. Make a total of 120 of these triangle-pieced squares. At this point, the triangle-pieced squares should measure $3\frac{1}{2}$ inches square.

Diagram 3

4 To make each of the six stem units for Leaf Block A, center a $3\frac{1}{2}$-inch beige triangle on a $1\frac{1}{4}$ × 6-inch green strip, as shown at the top left of **Diagram 4.** Stitch a $\frac{1}{4}$-inch seam, as shown, and press. Repeat on the other side of the green strip, as shown at top right in the diagram. Press the seam allowances toward the stem.

NOTE: *The green stems will extend beyond the beige triangles. Square off the stem units to $3\frac{1}{2}$ inches square, making sure the stem is centered.*

Diagram 4

Plan Ahead

Consider cutting the binding strips *before* you start piecing a large quilt like Fall Colors. That way, you can avoid misplacing or using the binding fabric for something else. You can also prepare the binding ahead of time by sewing all of the strips together, pressing the binding in half, and wrapping it around a magazine to keep it flat and wrinkle-free. Write the name of the quilt on a piece of masking tape, put it on the magazine, and your binding will be easy to locate when you need it.

5 To make the 12 stem units for Leaf Block B, repeat Step 4, using the 3½-inch beige triangles and the 1¼ × 6-inch red floral strips, as shown in **Diagram 5.**

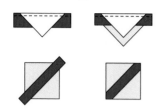

Diagram 5

6 Each Leaf Block A contains one stem unit, two 3½-inch beige squares, one 3½-inch green square, one 6½-inch green square, and eight 3½-inch green and beige triangle-pieced squares. Referring to **Diagram 6,** sew the block together in rows, and press. Make a total of six of Leaf Block A. At this point, Leaf Block A should measure 12½ inches square.

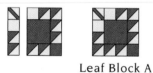

Leaf Block A

Diagram 6

7 Each Leaf Block B contains one stem unit, one 3½-inch beige square, one 6½-inch red floral square, and ten 3½-inch red floral and beige triangle-pieced squares. Referring to **Diagram 7,** sew the block together in rows, and press. Make a total of 12 of Leaf Block B. At this point, Leaf Block B should measure 12½ inches square.

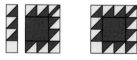

Leaf Block B

Diagram 7

SQUARE BLOCK C

(Make 17)

Cutting

From the gold print fabric:

✦ Cut three 6½ × 44-inch strips

From the red print fabric:

✦ Cut twelve 3½ × 44-inch strips. From these strips, cut thirty-four 3½ × 12½-inch rectangles.

✦ Cut six more 3½ × 44-inch strips to be used in the Step 1 strip sets.

Piecing

1 Sew the 3½ × 44-inch red strips to both sides of the three 6½ × 44-inch gold strips, as shown in **Diagram 8,** and press. Cross cut the strip sets into seventeen 6½-inch-wide segments, as shown.

6½"

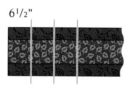

Diagram 8

2 Sew the 3½ × 12½-inch red rectangles to both sides of the Step 1 segments, as shown in **Diagram 9.** At this point, each Square Block C should measure 12½ inches square.

Diagram 9

QUILT CENTER

1 Sew together four block rows, as shown in **Diagram 10,** and press the seam allowances toward the Square C Blocks.

Diagram 10

2 Sew together three block rows, as shown in **Diagram 11,** and press the seam allowances toward the Square C Blocks.

Diagram 11

3 Referring to the **Quilt Diagram** on page 27, sew the block rows together to form the quilt center, and press.

BORDERS

The yardage given allows for the border strips to be cut on the crosswise grain. The border strips are longer than necessary and will be trimmed later.

Cutting

From the green print fabric:

✦ Cut eight 3½ × 44-inch strips for the inner border

From the red floral fabric:

✦ Cut nine 6½ × 44-inch strips for the middle border

✦ Cut ten 3½ × 44-inch strips for the outer border

From the gold print fabric:

✦ Cut four 6½-inch corner squares

Quilt Diagram

Attaching the Borders

1 To attach the 3½-inch-wide green inner border strips, as shown in the **Quilt Diagram,** refer to "Border Instructions" on page 198.

2 To attach the top and bottom 6½-inch-wide red floral middle border strips, as shown in the **Quilt Diagram,** refer to page 198 for "Border Instructions."

3 To attach the side 6½-inch-wide red floral middle border strips with gold corner squares, as shown in the **Quilt Diagram,** refer to "Borders with Corner Squares" on page 200.

4 To attach the 3½-inch-wide red floral outer border strips, as shown in the **Quilt Diagram,** refer to page 198 for "Border Instructions."

PUTTING IT ALL TOGETHER

1 Cut the 7½-yard length of backing fabric in thirds crosswise to make three 2½-yard lengths. Remove the selvages and sew the long edges together. Press the seam allowances open. Trim the backing and batting so they are about 4 inches larger than the quilt top.

2 For quilting ideas, see the **Quilting Design Diagram.** See page 201 for detailed marking, layering, and finishing instructions.

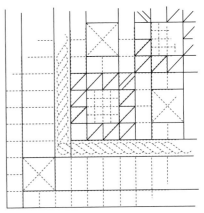

Quilting Design Diagram

BINDING

The 2¾-inch binding strips will produce a ½-inch-wide finished binding. If you want a wider or narrower binding, adjust the width of the strips you cut. (See page 201 for pointers on how to experiment with binding width.) Refer to "Attaching Binding with Mitered Corners" on page 202 to complete your quilt.

Cutting Crosswise Strips

From the green print binding fabric:
✦ Cut ten 2¾ × 44-inch strips on the crosswise grain

Fabric-Trimmed Rug

FABRICS AND SUPPLIES

✦ Small purchased rug

✦ Coordinating fabric for trim

1 Measure the width of your rug, and add 4 inches to this measurement.

2 Cut two 18-inch-wide pieces of a coordinating fabric to the length determined in Step 1.

3 Fold the fabric in half, wrong sides together, with the long, raw edges aligned, as shown in **Diagram 1,** and press.

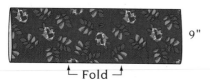

9"

L Fold ⌐

Diagram 1

4 Place the folded fabric trim on the rug, aligning the long, raw edges with each end of the rug, as shown in **Diagram 2.** Allow 2 inches of fabric to extend beyond each side of the rug, as shown.

2³/₄"

2"

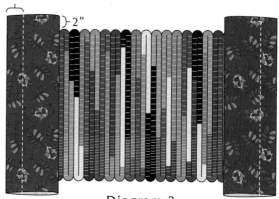

Diagram 2

5 Referring to **Diagram 2,** mark a stitching line 2¾ inches from the raw edge of the fabric trim. Stitch through both layers of the fabric trim and the rug, using a longer than average stitch, such as five or six stitches per inch. The stitch length may be determined by the thickness of your rug and your sewing machine's ability to feed and stitch through it. Stitch slowly so you can control all thicknesses.

6 Bring the fabric trim over the edge of the rug to the other side. Fold in the raw edges, and hand stitch the ends and the folded edge of the fabric trim to the rug. Repeat at the other end of the rug.

Kathie Haddock
Nurse

My Life When I'm Not Quilting

I've been a nurse for 30 years and value the role I play in helping patients go through the process of healing. My current work with chronically ill patients at an internal medicine clinic enables me to have a schedule of daytime hours with weekends free, which allows me more time for family activities.

Why I Quilt

Caring for people who are recovering from serious illnesses can be both demanding and stressful. After a long day, quilting is a wonderful way to relax and feel refreshed. Quilting will always be my favorite therapy and relief from the stresses of daily living.

My Most Memorable Project

Last year, I participated in a quiltmaking class held outdoors at a barn on a warm summer day. We each selected several block patterns from *The Thimbleberries Book of Quilts*, and Lynette Jensen showed us how to set them together to create totally unique quilts. I made a twin-size quilt that I've loved ever since, because it was truly my own creation.

My Best Tip for Finding More Time for Quilting

Go on group getaways! Six of my friends and I call ourselves the "Cabin Quilters," because we love to travel to a friend's cabin in the country for one weekend every other month to enjoy uninterrupted stitching time.

The colors you like most are an expression of yourself—they make a quilt your own and give it your unique personality.

—Kathie Haddock

My Favorite Things

Size

Wall Quilt: 51 × 64 inches (unquilted)

Fabrics and Supplies

Yardage is based on 44-inch-wide fabric.

- ¼ yard red print #1 fabric for quilt center
- ¼ yard red print #2 fabric for quilt center
- ¼ yard black print #1 fabric for quilt center
- ¼ yard brown plaid fabric for quilt center
- ½ yard brown print #1 fabric for quilt center
- ½ yard blue plaid fabric for quilt center
- ¼ yard green print fabric for quilt center
- ½ yard green plaid fabric for quilt center
- ½ yard brown print #2 fabric for inner border
- ½ yard black print #2 fabric for middle border and corner squares
- 1¾ yards red-chestnut-blue plaid fabric for outer border
- Assortment of red, green, brown, and white fat quarters for appliqués
- 2 yards paper-backed fusible web
- One spool #8 DMC gold pearl cotton
- One spool #8 DMC black pearl cotton
- ⅝ yard black print #2 fabric for binding
- 3⅓ yards fabric for quilt backing
- Quilt batting, at least 55 × 68 inches
- Rotary cutter, mat, and wide see-through ruler with ⅛-inch markings

Color Play

See page 32 for a creative color variation on the quilt shown here.

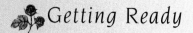 *Getting Ready*

- Read instructions thoroughly before you begin.

- Note that the appliqué in this project is done using the fusible appliqué method.

- Prewash and press fabric.

- Place right sides of fabric pieces together and use ¼-inch seam allowances throughout unless directions specify otherwise.

- Seam allowances are included in the cutting sizes given.

- Press seam allowances in the direction that will create the least bulk, and whenever possible, press toward the darker fabric. Press border seam allowances toward the borders unless directions specify otherwise.

- Cutting directions for each section of the quilt are given individually. If you like to cut as you go, simply follow the directions as you get to them. If you'd rather cut all your pieces at the same time, skip ahead to find each of the cutting sections and do all the cutting before you begin.

FABRIC KEY
(for the quilt shown on page 31)

Red #1	Red #2	Black #1
Brown plaid	Brown #1	Blue plaid
Green print	Green plaid	Brown #2
Black #2	Red-chestnut-blue plaid	

 **Color Play**

This smaller version of My Favorite Things proves that bigger isn't always better. The stars, snowflakes, and reindeer appliqués in the larger quilt are just as effective when sprinkled over a smaller background of blue prints and plaids—and the result is a quilt you'll love displaying all year round.

QUILT CENTER

Cutting

From the red print #1 fabric:
- Cut one 6½ × 10½-inch rectangle
- Cut one 6½ × 12½-inch rectangle

From the red print #2 fabric:
- Cut one 6½ × 22½-inch rectangle

From the black print #1 fabric:
- Cut one 6½ × 15½-inch rectangle

From the brown plaid fabric:
- Cut one 6½ × 10½-inch rectangle
- Cut one 6½ × 22½-inch rectangle

From the brown print #1 fabric:
- Cut one 13½ × 18½-inch rectangle

From the blue plaid fabric:
- Cut one 12½ × 29½-inch rectangle

From the green print fabric:
- Cut one 6½ × 22½-inch rectangle
- Cut one 6½ × 12½-inch rectangle

From the green plaid fabric:
- Cut one 12½ × 29½-inch rectangle

Appliquéing

Where indicated, some of the appliqué pattern pieces on pages 35–39 are reversed for tracing purposes, so they will appear in the correct positions when stitched. Follow the tracing instructions provided on each pattern piece.

1 Position the fusible web (paper side up) over the appliqué shapes on pages 35–39. Trace 14 A Stars, 7 small B Snowflakes, 3 large C Snowflakes, 9 D Holly Leaves, 9 E Holly Berries, 1 F Sleigh, 1 G Tree and 1 H Base, 2 I Mittens and 2 J Cuffs, and 2 K Reindeer onto the fusible web, leaving at least ½ inch between each shape.

2 Roughly cut around the shapes, outside your traced lines, as shown in **Diagram 1.**

NOTE: *When you are fusing a large shape, like the Mitten, fuse just the outer edges of the shape, so that it will not look stiff when finished. To do this, draw a line about ⅜ inch inside the Mitten, and cut away the fusible web on this line, as shown.*

Cut away

Diagram 1

3 Following the manufacturer's instructions, fuse the shapes to the wrong side of the fabrics you have selected, as shown in **Diagram 2.** Let the fabric cool, and cut along the outline of each shape, as

shown. Peel away the paper from the fusible web.

Wrong side of fabric

Diagram 2

4 Referring to the **Quilt Diagram** on page 34, position the appliqués on the appropriate rectangles and fuse them in place. Make sure to place each appliqué at least ¼ inch from the edge of the rectangles, to allow for seam allowances. Wait to position the two snowflake appliqués that overlap seam lines until after you have assembled the quilt center.

Plan Ahead

To save time, plan to do various tasks in stages. For example, cut all of the background pieces for My Favorite Things at the same time. Trace all of the appliqués onto fusible web in one sitting. Fuse all of the shapes onto the background pieces on the same day. That way, you'll always have something prepared and ready to stitch at a moment's notice whenever your schedule allows.

Quilt Diagram

5 Using the buttonhole stitch and one strand of pearl cotton, appliqué the shapes in place. Refer to page 197 for "Decorative Stitches."

Assembly

1 Referring to the **Quilt Diagram,** sew the appliquéd rectangles together in horizontal rows, and press. Sew the rows together to form the quilt center, and press.

Tuck some prepared appliqué blocks, coordinating threads, and needles for My Favorite Things into a Ziploc bag, and keep the bag in your car. It's amazing how much stitching you can accomplish while waiting in a doctor's office, or anywhere you have a few spare moments away from home.

2 Referring to the **Quilt Diagram,** fuse a small B Snowflake over the seam line between the blue plaid and the black #1 rectangles at the top of the quilt. In the same manner, fuse a large C Snowflake over the seam line between the green print and the brown plaid rectangles at the left side of the quilt, as shown. Use the buttonhole stitch and one strand of pearl cotton to appliqué the snowflakes in place.

BORDERS

The yardage given allows for the inner and middle border strips to be cut on the crosswise grain, and the outer border strips to be cut lengthwise. The borders are longer than necessary and will be trimmed later.

Cutting

From the brown print #2 fabric:

✦ Cut five 2½ × 44-inch strips for the inner border

From the black print #2 fabric:

✦ Cut five 1½ × 44-inch strips for the middle border

✦ Cut four 5½-inch corner squares

From the red-chestnut-blue plaid fabric, on the lengthwise grain:

✦ Cut two 5½ × 45-inch strips for the top and bottom outer border

✦ Cut two 5½ × 58-inch strips for the side outer border

Attaching the Borders

1 To attach the 2½-inch-wide brown inner border strips, as shown in the **Quilt Diagram,** refer to page 198 for "Border Instructions."

2 To attach the 1½-inch-wide black middle border strips, as shown in the **Quilt Diagram,** refer to page 198 for "Border Instructions."

3 To attach the 5½-inch-wide plaid top and bottom outer border strips, as shown in the **Quilt Diagram,** refer to page 198 for "Border Instructions."

4 To attach the 5½-inch-wide plaid side border strips with black corner squares, as shown in the **Quilt Diagram,** refer to page 200 for "Borders with Corner Squares."

PUTTING IT ALL TOGETHER

1 Cut the 3⅓-yard length of backing fabric in half crosswise to make two 1⅔-yard lengths. Remove the selvages and sew the long edges together. Press the seam allowances open. Trim the backing and batting so they are about 4 inches larger than the quilt top.

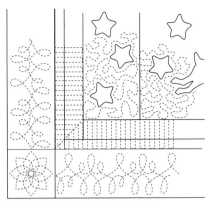

Quilting Design Diagram

2 For quilting ideas, see the **Quilting Design Diagram.** See page 201 for detailed marking, layering, and finishing instructions.

BINDING

The 2¾-inch binding strips will produce a ½-inch-wide finished binding. If you want a wider or narrower binding, adjust the width of the strips you cut. (See page 201 for pointers on how to experiment with binding width.) Refer to "Attaching Binding with Mitered Corners" on page 202 to complete your quilt.

Cutting Crosswise Strips

From the black print #2 binding fabric:

✦ Cut six 2¾ × 44-inch strips on the crosswise grain

C
Snowflake
(TRACE 3)

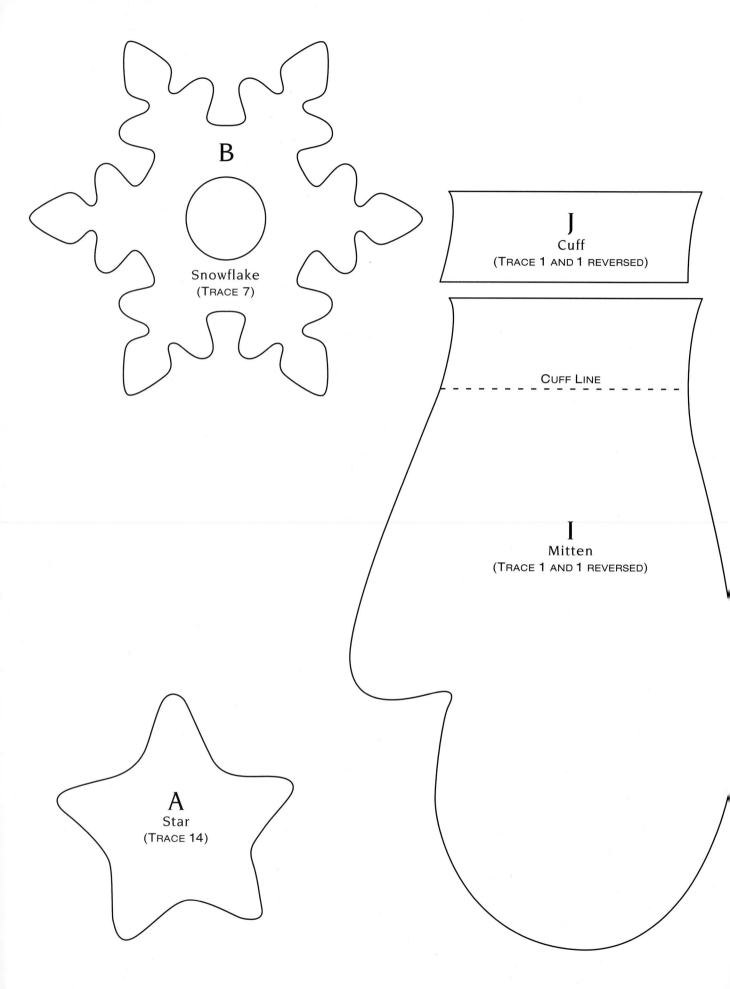

B

Snowflake
(TRACE 7)

J
Cuff
(TRACE 1 AND 1 REVERSED)

CUFF LINE

I
Mitten
(TRACE 1 AND 1 REVERSED)

A
Star
(TRACE 14)

MY • FAVORITE • THINGS

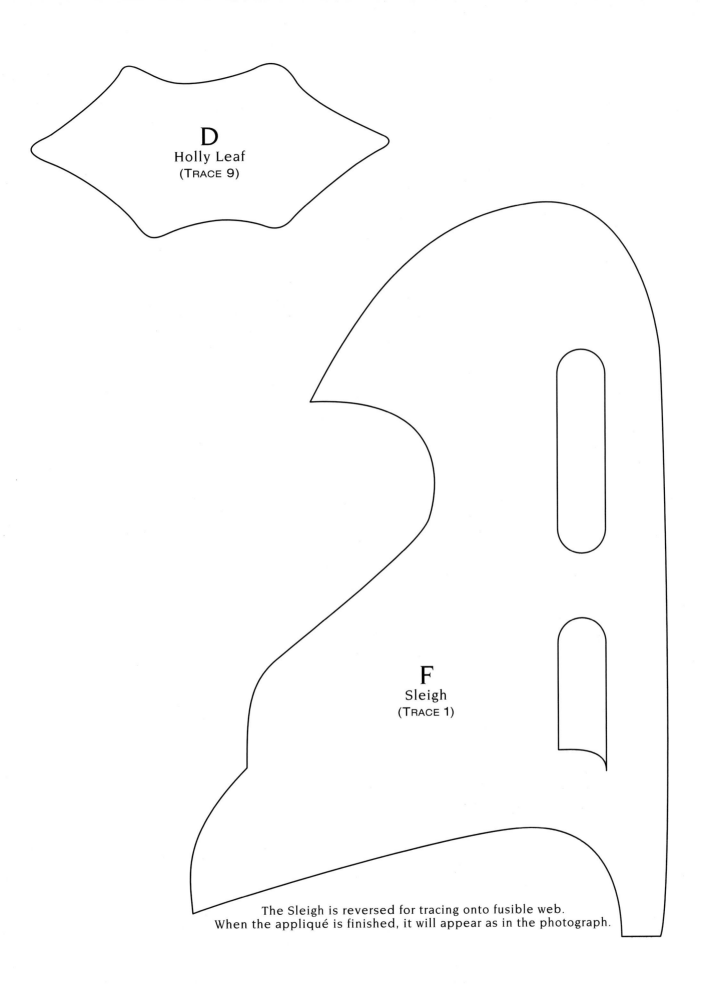

D
Holly Leaf
(TRACE 9)

F
Sleigh
(TRACE 1)

The Sleigh is reversed for tracing onto fusible web.
When the appliqué is finished, it will appear as in the photograph.

E
Holly Berry
(TRACE 9)

G
Tree
(TRACE 1)

OVERLAP

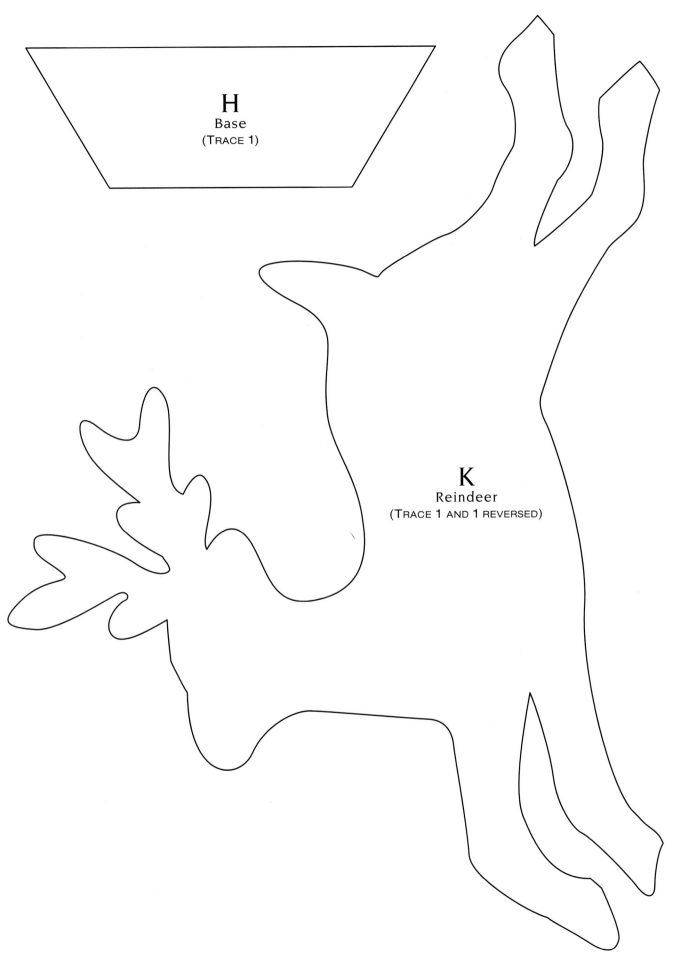

H
Base
(TRACE 1)

K
Reindeer
(TRACE 1 AND 1 REVERSED)

SLICE OF SUMMER TABLE RUNNER

MAKE IT TONIGHT

SIZE

Table Runner: 30 × 36 inches (unquilted)

HOUSE  DRESSING

See the Stenciled Ice Bucket on top of the runner on the buffet. Directions are given on page 45.

FABRICS AND SUPPLIES

Yardage is based on 44-inch-wide fabric.

- ½ yard green print #1 fabric for Checkerboard Center
- ¾ yard pink print fabric for Checkerboard Center and Pieced Border
- ⅜ yard beige print fabric for Pieced Border
- ⅝ yard green print #2 fabric for outer border
- 9 × 18-inch rectangle green print #3 fabric for watermelon appliqués
- ¾ yard pink plaid fabric for watermelon appliqués and bias binding
- ½ yard paper-backed fusible web
- One spool #8 DMC black pearl cotton
- 1 yard fabric for quilt backing
- Quilt batting, at least 34 × 40 inches
- Rotary cutter, mat, and wide see-through ruler with ⅛-inch markings

Color Play

See page 42 for a creative color variation on the quilt shown here.

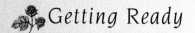 *Getting Ready*

� Read instructions thoroughly before you begin.

✀ Note that the appliqué in this project is done using the fusible appliqué method.

✀ Prewash and press fabric.

✀ Place right sides of fabric pieces together and use ¼-inch seam allowances throughout unless directions specify otherwise.

✀ Seam allowances are included in the cutting sizes given.

✀ Press seam allowances in the direction that will create the least bulk, and whenever possible, press toward the darker fabric. Press border seam allowances toward the borders unless directions specify otherwise.

✀ Cutting directions for each section of the quilt are given individually. If you like to cut as you go, simply follow the directions as you get to them. If you'd rather cut all your pieces at the same time, skip ahead to find each of the cutting sections and do all the cutting before you begin.

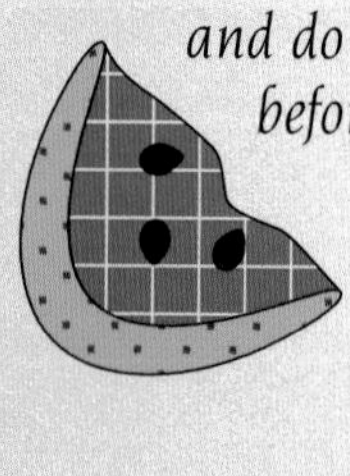

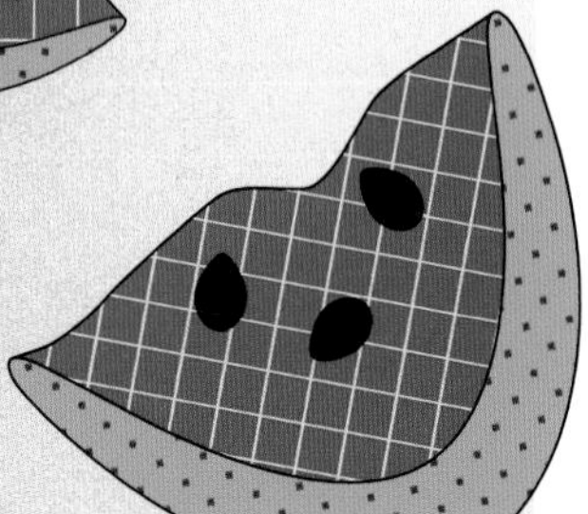

FABRIC KEY
(for the quilt shown on page 41)

Green #1   Pink print

Beige   Green #2   Green #3   Pink plaid

Color Play

I chose a pumpkin-and-black Checkerboard Center and medium green border to transform Slice of Summer Table Runner into a hint of Halloween. And without the watermelon appliqués, this quilt takes on a distinctive, new look that would complement any autumn decor.

CHECKERBOARD CENTER

Cutting

From the green print #1 fabric:
✦ Cut three 3½ × 44-inch strips

From the pink print fabric:
✦ Cut three 3½ × 44-inch strips

Piecing

1 Sew the 3½ × 44-inch green and pink strips together in pairs, as shown in **Diagram 1,** and press. Make a total of three strip sets and cross cut them into twenty-four 3½-inch segments, as shown.

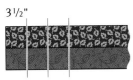

3½"

Diagram 1

2 Sew six segments together in a row, alternating colors as shown in **Diagram 2,** and press. Make four of these rows and sew them together to make the Checkerboard Center, and press. At this point, the Checkerboard Center should measure 18½ × 24½ inches.

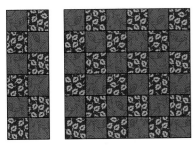

Diagram 2

PIECED BORDER

Cutting

From the pink print fabric:
✦ Cut three 3½ × 44-inch strips. From these strips, cut thirty-two 3½-inch squares.

From the beige print fabric:
✦ Cut three 3½ × 44-inch strips. From these strips, cut fourteen 3½ × 6½-inch rectangles.

Piecing

1 Position a 3½-inch pink square on the corner of each 3½ × 6½-inch beige rectangle, as shown in **Diagram 3.** Draw a diagonal line on each pink square, as shown at left in the diagram, and stitch on this line. Trim the seam allowances to ¼ inch, and press, as shown at right.

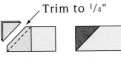

Trim to ¹/₄"

Diagram 3

2 Repeat this process on the opposite corner of each of the beige rectangles, as shown in **Diagram 4.**

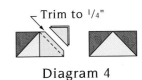

Trim to ¹/₄"

Diagram 4

3 Referring to the **Quilt Diagram,** sew four Step 2 units together to make the top and bottom borders, and press. Sew the top and bottom borders to the Checkerboard Center, and press.

4 Sew three Step 2 units together for each of the side borders, referring to the **Quilt Diagram.** Add a 3½-inch pink square to each end of these borders, referring to the diagram, and press. Sew these side borders to the Checkerboard Center, and press.

Quilt Diagram

OUTER BORDER

The yardage given allows for the border strips to be cut on the crosswise grain. The border strips are longer than necessary and will be trimmed later.

Cutting

From the green print #2 fabric:

✦ Cut four 3½ × 44-inch strips for the outer border

Attaching the Border

To attach the 3½-inch-wide green outer border, as shown in the **Quilt Diagram** on page 43, refer to page 198 for "Border Instructions."

APPLIQUÉING

Where indicated, some of the appliqué pattern pieces on page 45 are reversed for tracing purposes, so they will appear in the correct positions when stitched. Follow the tracing instructions provided on each pattern piece.

1 Position the fusible web (paper side up) over the watermelon shapes on page 45. Trace 5 A Watermelons, 5 B Rinds, and 15 C Seeds, taking care to leave at least ½ inch between traced shapes. Roughly cut out the pieces outside of the traced lines.

2 For the A Watermelons, draw a line approximately ⅜ inch inside your traced lines, as shown in **Diagram 5.** Cut away the fusible web from each shape on this drawn line, as shown.

NOTE: *When you fuse a large shape, like the A Watermelon, it is helpful to fuse only the outer edges of each shape. This will keep the watermelons from looking stiff and will also make it much easier to buttonhole stitch the seeds and rinds in place later.*

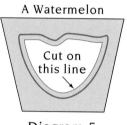

A Watermelon

Cut on this line

Diagram 5

3 With a hot, dry iron, press the coated side of the fusible web watermelon shapes to the wrong side of the fabrics chosen for the appliqués. Let the fabric cool, and cut out the watermelon shapes directly on your traced outlines. Peel off the paper backing.

4 Referring to the **Quilt Diagram** on page 43 for placement, position and fuse the A Watermelon shapes on the table runner, followed by the B Rinds and the C Seeds.

5 Using one strand of black pearl cotton, appliqué the watermelon pieces in place by hand with the buttonhole stitch. Refer to page 197 for "Decorative Stitches."

PUTTING IT ALL TOGETHER

1 Trim the backing and batting so they are about 4 inches larger than the table runner.

2 For quilting ideas, see the **Quilting Design Diagram.** See page 201 for marking, layering, and finishing instructions.

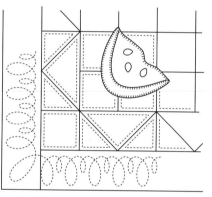

Quilting Design Diagram

BINDING

The 2¾-inch-wide plaid bias strips will produce a ½-inch-wide finished binding. If you would like a wider or narrower binding, adjust the width of the strips you cut. (See page 201 for pointers on how to experiment with binding width.) Refer to "Attaching Binding with Mitered Corners" on page 202 to complete your quilt.

Cutting Bias Strips

From the pink plaid fabric:

✦ Cut enough 2¾-inch bias strips to make a 150-inch-long binding strip

For Slice of Summer Table Runner, you can put together a great travel kit for hand stitching whenever you're on the go. Piece the table runner, add the fusible appliqué watermelon shapes to it, and pop it all into a plastic bag, along with some pearl cotton and a needle. That way, you can do the hand buttonhole stitching on car trips, during air travel, or while visiting friends or family.

Stenciled Ice Bucket

SUPPLIES

+ 3-gallon galvanized tin pail from hardware store

+ Latex paints and template plastic from hobby/craft store

+ Pink and green stencil paints for walls

+ Walnut wood stain (optional)

+ Acrylic matte finish spray

1 Paint one coat of cream latex paint on the outside and about 4 inches to the inside of your pail. Allow the paint to dry for 4 hours.

2 Cut the appliqué shapes below out of template plastic, *eliminating* the lower part of the watermelon flesh that lies underneath the rind when appliquéd.

3 Using the stencil paints, stencil the shapes on the pail, and allow the paints to dry for 24 hours.

4 To give the pail the mellow look of age, use the walnut wood stain and a rag to rub stain sparingly over the entire pail, and allow it to dry for 24 hours (optional).

5 To seal the surface, spray with acrylic matte finish.

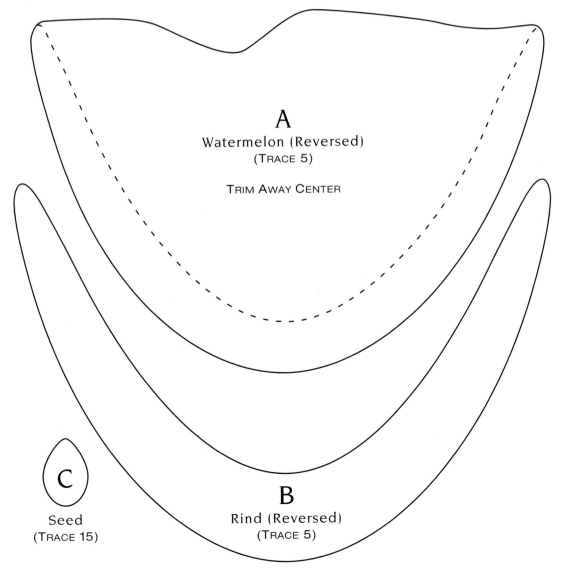

A
Watermelon (Reversed)
(TRACE 5)

TRIM AWAY CENTER

C
Seed
(TRACE 15)

B
Rind (Reversed)
(TRACE 5)

SPINNERS

MAKE
IT
TONIGHT

SIZE

Wall Quilt: 36 inches square (unquilted)

FABRICS AND SUPPLIES

Yardage is based on 44-inch-wide fabric.

+ ½ yard green print #1 fabric for Pinwheel Blocks

+ ½ yard red print fabric for Pinwheel Blocks

+ ⅝ yard beige floral fabric for Triangle Blocks

+ ⅝ yard beige print fabric for Triangle Blocks

+ 1 yard green print #2 fabric for border

+ ½ yard red print fabric for binding

+ 1¼ yards fabric for quilt backing

+ Quilt batting, at least 40 inches square

+ Rotary cutter, mat, and wide see-through ruler
  with ⅛-inch markings

Color Play

See page 48 for a creative color variation
on the quilt shown here.

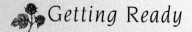 *Getting Ready*

- Read instructions thoroughly before you begin.

- Prewash and press fabric.

- Place right sides of fabric pieces together and use ¼-inch seam allowances throughout unless directions specify otherwise.

- Seam allowances are included in the cutting sizes given.

- Press seam allowances in the direction that will create the least bulk, and whenever possible, press toward the darker fabric. Press border seam allowances toward the borders unless directions specify otherwise.

- Cutting directions for each section of the quilt are given individually. If you like to cut as you go, simply follow the directions as you get to them. If you'd rather cut all your pieces at the same time, skip ahead to find each of the cutting sections and do all the cutting before you begin.

FABRIC KEY
(for the quilt shown on page 47)

| Green #1 | Red | Beige floral | Beige print | Green #2 |

Color Play

To create a more muted, subtle coloration than the Spinners quilt shown on page 47, I chose a deep, dark red for the border, dusty shades of blue and red for the Pinwheel Blocks, and a darker tan print for the Triangle Blocks for this quilt.

PINWHEEL BLOCKS

(Make 1 large
and 8 small)

Cutting

From the green print #1 fabric:

✦ Cut two 4⅞-inch squares

✦ Cut two 2⅞ × 44-inch strips. From these strips, cut sixteen 2⅞-inch squares.

From the red print fabric:

✦ Cut two 4⅞-inch squares

✦ Cut two 2⅞ × 44-inch strips. From these strips, cut sixteen 2⅞-inch squares.

Piecing

1 Layer a green and red 4⅞-inch square, as shown at the top of **Diagram 1.** Press them together, but do not sew. Cut the layered squares in half diagonally, and sew a ¼-inch seam along the diagonal edge, and press. Repeat with the remaining 4⅞-inch squares. Also, repeat this process with the 2⅞-inch squares, as shown at the bottom of the diagram.

Plan Ahead

To ward off back strain, sit in an adjustable office swivel chair while you are sewing. It offers the benefit of good back support, plus allows you to remain seated while turning to press pieces at a lowered ironing board.

Diagram 1

2 Sew the larger triangle-pieced squares together in pairs, as shown in **Diagram 2.** Sew these pairs together to form the large center Pinwheel Block, as shown. Sew the smaller triangle-pieced squares together in the same manner, as shown at right. Make a total of eight small Pinwheel Blocks. At this point, the small Pinwheel Blocks should measure 4½ inches square.

Diagram 2

TRIANGLE BLOCKS

(Make 12)

Cutting

From the beige floral fabric:

✦ Cut twelve 4½ × 8½-inch rectangles

From the beige print fabric:

✦ Cut twenty-four 4½-inch squares

Piecing

Position a 4½-inch beige square on the corner of a 4½ × 8½-inch floral rectangle, as shown at the top of **Diagram**

3. Stitch diagonally from corner to corner on the beige square, as shown. Trim the seam allowance to ¼ inch, and press. Repeat this process at the opposite corner of the floral rectangle, as shown at the bottom of the diagram. Make a total of 12 of these units.

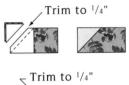
Trim to ¹/₄"

Trim to ¹/₄"

Diagram 3

QUILT CENTER

1 Referring to **Diagram 4,** sew a Triangle Block to the top and bottom of the large Pinwheel Block, and press. Sew small Pinwheel Blocks to each end of two Triangle Blocks, and press. Sew these units to the sides of the large Pinwheel Block, as shown, and press. At this point, the quilt center should measure 16½ inches square.

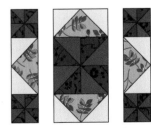

Diagram 4

2 Referring to the **Quilt Diagram** on page 50 for block placement, sew the remaining Triangle Blocks together in pairs, and sew these units to

Quilt Diagram

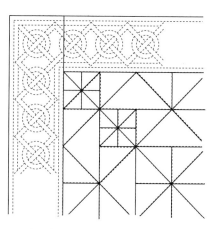

Quilting Design Diagram

the top and bottom of the quilt center, and press. Sew small Pinwheel Blocks to each end of the remaining units, and sew them to the sides of the quilt center, and press. At this point, the quilt center should measure 24½ inches square.

BORDER

The yardage given allows for the border strips to be cut on the crosswise grain. The border strips are longer than necessary and will be trimmed later.

Cutting

From the green print #2 fabric:

✦ Cut four 6½ × 44-inch strips

Attaching the Border

To attach the 6½-inch-wide green border strips as shown in the **Quilt Diagram,** refer to page 198 for "Border Instructions."

PUTTING IT ALL TOGETHER

1 Trim the backing and batting so they are about 4 inches larger than the quilt top.

2 For quilting ideas, see the **Quilting Design Diagram.** See page 201 for detailed marking, layering, and finishing instructions.

BINDING

The 2¾-inch binding strips will produce a ½-inch-wide finished binding. If you want a wider or narrower binding, adjust the width of the strips you cut. (See page 201 for pointers on how to experiment with binding width.) See "Attaching Binding with Mitered Corners" on page 202 to complete your quilt.

Cutting Crosswise Strips

From the red print binding fabric:

✦ Cut four 2¾ × 44-inch strips on the crosswise grain

Lisa Kirchoff
Graphic Artist and Designer, Thimbleberries, Inc.

My Life When I'm Not Quilting

Working at Thimbleberries, Inc., is a dream job for any quilter. My work involves doing graphics, illustrations, and diagrams; typing instructions; and designing pattern and book layouts and covers. One of the best parts of my job is being inspired by the creativity and the beautiful quilts I see daily in my professional surroundings.

Why I Quilt

In the five years since I've become a part of Thimbleberries, Inc., quilting has developed into an important part of my home life as well. Creating step-by-step quilt diagrams at work makes it very easy to start visualizing how different quilts would look in my house. I enjoy making lap quilts, wall quilts, and bed quilts, and I love the sense of warmth and comfort that comes from being surrounded at home by quilts and accessories I've made with my own hands.

My Best Tip for Finding More Time for Quilting

Stay up late! Thursday evenings are prime sewing time at my house, because I don't work on Fridays. I often quilt till 1:00 or 2:00 A.M.—late nights are great—my children are asleep, the house is quiet, the phone is silent, and there are no further demands on my time. And after getting the kids off to school the next morning, Friday is always a great day for relaxing.

> *Seeing the joy in people's eyes when they receive a quilt I've made especially for them is something I wouldn't ever want to give up.*
>
> —Lisa Kirchoff

STARBURST TABLE RUNNER

SIZE

Table Runner: 24 × 52 inches (unquilted)
Finished Block: 12 inches square

HOUSE DRESSING

See the Napkins and Ties on the table runner.
Directions are given on page 57.

FABRICS AND SUPPLIES

Yardage is based on 44-inch-wide fabric.

- ✦ ¼ yard gold print fabric for Star Block centers and corner posts

- ✦ ⅝ yard red print fabric for Star Blocks and corner squares

- ✦ ⅔ yard dark red print fabric for Star Blocks and lattice

- ✦ 1 yard beige print fabric for Star Block background and borders

- ✦ ½ yard dark red print fabric for binding

- ✦ 1⅝ yards fabric for quilt backing

- ✦ Quilt batting, at least 28 × 56 inches

- ✦ Rotary cutter, mat, and wide see-through ruler with ⅛-inch markings

Color Play

See page 54 for a creative color variation
on the quilt shown here.

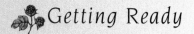 Getting Ready

- Read instructions thoroughly before you begin.

- Prewash and press fabric.

- Place right sides of fabric pieces together and use ¼-inch seam allowances throughout unless directions specify otherwise.

- Seam allowances are included in the cutting sizes given.

- Press seam allowances in the direction that will create the least bulk, and whenever possible, press toward the darker fabric. Press border seam allowances toward the borders unless directions specify otherwise.

- Cutting directions for each section of the quilt are given individually. If you like to cut as you go, simply follow the directions as you get to them. If you'd rather cut all your pieces at the same time, skip ahead to find each of the cutting sections and do all the cutting before you begin.

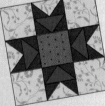

| Gold | Red | Dark red | Beige |

Color Play

For this color variation table runner, I decided on a soft blue floral and a lighter red print to take the place of the dark red in the stars in the Starburst quilt on page 53. When combined with lattice strips in the same cheerful red, the overall effect of this color variation is both bright and lively.

STAR BLOCKS

(Make 3)

Cutting

From the gold print fabric:
✦ Cut three 4½-inch squares

From the red print fabric:
✦ Cut three 2½ × 44-inch strips. From these strips, cut forty-eight 2½-inch squares.

From the dark red print fabric:
✦ Cut two 2½ × 44-inch strips. From these strips, cut twelve 2½ × 4½-inch rectangles.

From the beige print fabric:
✦ Cut two 2½ × 44-inch strips. From these strips, cut twelve 2½ × 4½-inch rectangles.

✦ Cut two 4½ × 44-inch strips. From these strips, cut twelve 4½-inch squares.

Piecing

1 Position a 2½-inch red square on the corner of a 2½ × 4½-inch dark red rectangle, as shown at the top of **Diagram 1.** Stitch diagonally from corner to corner on the red square, as shown. Trim the seam allowance to ¼ inch, and press. Repeat this process at the opposite corner of the dark red rectangle, as shown at the bottom of the diagram. Make a total of 12 of these star point units.

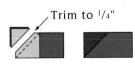
Trim to ¼"

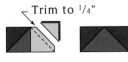
Trim to ¼"

Diagram 1

2 In the same manner, position and sew 2½-inch red squares on the corners of the 2½ × 4½-inch beige rectangles, as shown in **Diagram 2.** Make a total of 12 of these star point units.

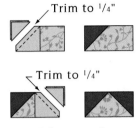
Trim to ¼"

Trim to ¼"

Diagram 2

3 Sew the Step 1 and 2 star point units together in pairs, positioning the Step 2 units on top, as shown in **Diagram 3,** and press.

Diagram 3

4 Sew the Step 3 units to the top and bottom of the 4½-inch gold squares, as shown in **Diagram 4,** and press.

Diagram 4

5 Referring to **Diagram 5,** sew the 4½-inch beige squares to both sides of the remaining

Step 3 units, and press. Sew these units to both sides of the Step 4 unit, as shown, and press. Make a total of three Star Blocks. At this point, the Star Blocks should measure 12½ inches square.

Diagram 5

To make your sewing time more efficient, keep a small pair of scissors, a small see-through ruler, a rotary cutter, and a small cutting mat near your machine for measuring, cutting, and trimming seam extensions.

QUILT CENTER

Cutting

From the dark red print fabric:
✦ Cut four 2½ × 44-inch strips. From these strips, cut ten 2½ × 12½-inch lattice pieces.

From the gold print fabric:
✦ Cut one 2½ × 44-inch strip. From this strip, cut eight 2½-inch square lattice posts.

Assembly

1 Sew together three 2½ × 12½-inch dark red lattice pieces and four 2½-inch square gold lattice posts for each lattice strip, as shown in **Diagram 6.** Press the seam allowances toward the lattice pieces.

2 Sew together the three Star Blocks and four 2½ × 12½-inch dark red lattice pieces, as shown in **Diagram 7.** Press the

seam allowances toward the lattice pieces.

3 Sew the Step 1 lattice strips to both sides of the row of Star Blocks, as shown in **Diagram 8.** Press the seam allowances toward the lattice strips.

Diagram 6

Diagram 7

Diagram 8

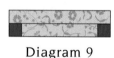

Diagram 9

Diagram 10

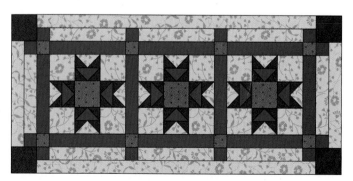

Quilt Diagram

BORDERS

The yardage given allows for the border strips to be cut on the crosswise grain. The border strips are longer than necessary and will be trimmed later.

Cutting

From the beige print fabric:

✦ Cut three 2½ × 44-inch strips. From these strips, cut eight 2½ × 12½-inch strips.

✦ Cut one more 2½ × 44-inch strip. From this strip, cut two 2½ × 16½-inch strips.

✦ Cut three more 2½ × 44-inch strips

From the dark red print fabric:

✦ Cut one 2½ × 44-inch strip. From this strip, cut twelve 2½-inch square lattice posts.

From the red print fabric:

✦ Cut four 4½-inch corner squares

Piecing and Attaching the Borders

1 Referring to **Diagram 9,** sew 2½-inch dark red squares to both ends of two of the 2½ × 12½-inch beige strips, and press. Sew the 2½ × 16½-inch beige strips to these strips, as shown, and press. Sew the pieced border units to the short ends of the runner center, as shown in the **Quilt Diagram,** and press.

2 Referring to **Diagram 10,** sew three 2½ × 12½-inch beige strips and four 2½-inch dark red lattice posts together. Press the seam allowances toward the lattice posts. Make two of these units.

3 Diagonally piece three 2½ × 44-inch beige strips together. Cut two 2½ × 44½-inch strips and sew them to the Step 2 units, referring to **Diagram 10,** and press. Sew the 4½-inch red corner squares to the ends of these units, as shown, and press.

4 Sew the Step 3 border units to the top and bottom of the table runner, referring to the **Quilt Diagram** on page 56, and press.

PUTTING IT ALL TOGETHER

1 Trim the backing and batting so they are about 4 inches larger than the quilt top.

2 For quilting ideas, see the **Quilting Design Diagram.** See page 201 for detailed marking, layering, and finishing instructions.

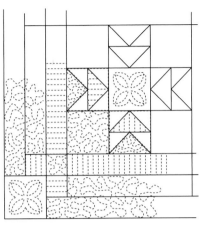

Quilting Design Diagram

BINDING

The 2¾-inch binding strips will produce a ½-inch-wide finished binding. If you want a wider or narrower binding, adjust the width of the strips you cut. (See page 201 for pointers on how to experiment with binding width.) Refer to "Attaching Binding with Mitered Corners" on page 202 to complete your quilt.

Cutting Crosswise Strips

From the dark red print binding fabric:

✦ Cut four 2¾ × 44-inch strips on the crosswise grain

HOUSE DRESSING
Napkins and Ties

FABRICS AND SUPPLIES
(for 4 napkins and ties)

✦ Four 18-inch squares cream and black checked fabric

✦ Four 5½ × 25-inch strips brown plaid fabric

1 To make the napkins, pull out enough threads along all four edges of the 18-inch squares of checked fabric to create ⅜-inch fringe on all sides.

2 To make the ties, fold the 5½ × 25-inch brown plaid strips in half lengthwise, with right sides together, and finger press.

3 Cut both ends of each tie at the same 45 degree angle, as shown in **Diagram 1.** Stitch ¼ inch

from the cut edges, leaving 3 inches open at the center, as shown.

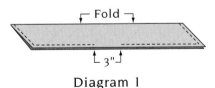

Diagram 1

4 Clip the corners, turn each of the ties right side out, and press, taking care to see that the corner angles are sharp and even.

5 Hand stitch the opening closed on each tie. Tie each one around a napkin folded loosely into a triangle.

WELCOME HOME

SIZE

Wall Quilt: 54 inches square (unquilted)
Finished Blocks: 12 inches square

 ## HOUSE DRESSING

See the Framed Block on the easel.
Directions are given on page 64.

FABRICS AND SUPPLIES

Yardage is based on 44-inch-wide fabric.

+ ⅞ yard red print fabric for houses and pieced inner border

+ ¼ yard black print fabric for chimneys

+ ½ yard brown print fabric for roofs

+ ¼ yard gold print fabric for windows

+ 1¼ yards beige print fabric for house and star background

+ 1 yard chestnut print fabric for stars and pieced inner border

+ 1 yard green floral fabric for pieced inner border and
outer border

+ ⅝ yard green floral fabric for binding

+ 3⅓ yards fabric for quilt backing

+ Quilt batting, at least 58 inches square

+ Rotary cutter, mat, and wide see-through ruler
with ⅛-inch markings

Color Play

See page 60 for a creative color variation
on the quilt shown here.

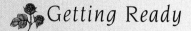

Getting Ready

* Read instructions thoroughly before you begin.

* Prewash and press fabric.

* Place right sides of fabric pieces together and use ¼-inch seam allowances throughout unless directions specify otherwise.

* Seam allowances are included in the cutting sizes given.

* Press seam allowances in the direction that will create the least bulk, and whenever possible, press toward the darker fabric. Press border seam allowances toward the borders unless directions specify otherwise.

* Cutting directions for each section of the quilt are given individually. If you like to cut as you go, simply follow the directions as you get to them. If you'd rather cut all your pieces at the same time, skip ahead to find each of the cutting sections and do all the cutting before you begin.

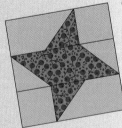

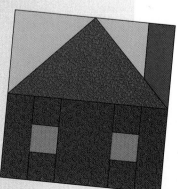

FABRIC KEY
(for the quilt shown on page 59)

Red   Black   Brown

Gold   Beige   Chestnut   Green floral

Color Play

The deep, rich colors of the Welcome Home quilt on page 59 take a different form in this quilt. I chose blue and red for the houses, a lighter gold for the stars, and a lighter beige for the background. With a colorful floral print in the border, the overall effect in this color variation is bright and inviting.

HOUSE BLOCKS

(Make 5)

Cutting

From the red print fabric:

◆ Cut two 2½ × 44-inch strips. From these strips, cut ten 2½ × 6½-inch rectangles.

◆ Cut two more 2½ × 44-inch strips, to be used in the Step 1 strip set.

◆ Cut one 4½ × 44-inch strip. From this strip, cut five 4½ × 6½-inch rectangles.

From the black print fabric:

◆ Cut one 2½ × 44-inch strip. From this strip, cut five 2½ × 6½-inch rectangles.

From the brown print fabric:

◆ Cut two 6½ × 44-inch strips. From these strips, cut five 6½ × 12½-inch rectangles.

From the gold print fabric:

◆ Cut one 2½ × 44-inch strip

From the beige print fabric:

◆ Cut two 6½ × 44-inch strips. From these strips, cut five 6½-inch squares and five 4½ × 6½-inch rectangles.

Piecing

1 Sew a 2½ × 44-inch red strip to both sides of the 2½ × 44-inch gold strip, as shown in **Diagram 1,** and press. Cut ten 2½-inch-wide segments from this strip set, as shown.

2½"

Diagram 1

2 Sew a Step 1 segment to both sides of each of the 4½ × 6½-inch red rectangles, as shown in **Diagram 2,** and press. Sew the 2½ × 6½-inch red rectangles to the sides of these units, as shown.

Diagram 2

3 Position a 6½-inch beige square on the left corner of each 6½ × 12½-inch brown rectangle, as shown at the top of **Diagram 3.** Draw a diagonal line on the beige square, as shown, and stitch on this line. Trim away the excess fabric, leaving a ¼-inch seam allowance, and press, as shown at the bottom.

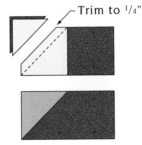

Trim to ¼"

Diagram 3

4 Sew the 2½ × 6½-inch black rectangles and the 4½ × 6½-inch beige rectangles together, as shown in **Diagram 4,** and press.

Diagram 4

5 Position a Step 4 unit on the right corner of each Step 3 unit, as shown at the top of

Diagram 5. Draw a diagonal line on the square unit, as shown, and stitch on this line. Trim away the excess fabric, leaving a ¼-inch seam allowance, and press, as shown at the bottom.

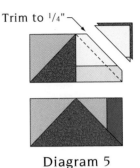

Trim to ¼"

Diagram 5

6 Sew the roof and house base units together, as shown in **Diagram 6,** and press. Make a total of five House Blocks. At this point, the House Blocks should measure 12½ inches square.

Diagram 6

Plan Ahead

Using a rotary cutter, mat, and ruler to trim the seam allowances on layered squares or rectangles to ¼ inch will yield pairs of perfectly shaped, smaller triangles. Don't throw them away! Instead, chain stitch these pairs together! You'll end up with lots of colorful triangle-pieced squares to keep on hand for Sawtooth Borders, Pinwheel Blocks, or other projects.

STAR BLOCKS

(Make 20)

Cutting

From the chestnut print fabric:

✦ Cut six 2½ × 44-inch strips. From these strips, cut twenty 2½ × 6½-inch rectangles and forty 2½-inch squares.

From the beige print fabric:

✦ Cut ten 2½ × 44-inch strips. From these strips, cut forty 2½ × 4½-inch rectangles and eighty 2½-inch squares.

Piecing

1 Position 2½-inch beige squares on the corners of the 2½ × 6½-inch chestnut rectangles, as shown at left in **Diagram 7.** Draw diagonal lines on the beige squares, as shown, and stitch on these lines. Trim away the excess fabric, leaving a ¼-inch seam allowance, and press, as shown at right. Make 20 of these units.

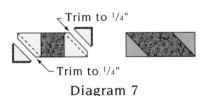

Trim to ¼"
Trim to ¼"

Diagram 7

2 Position a 2½-inch chestnut square on the corner of each of the 2½ × 4½-inch beige rectangles, as shown at left in **Diagram 8.** Draw a diagonal line on the chestnut squares, as shown, and stitch on the line. Trim away the excess fabric, leaving a ¼-inch seam allowance, as shown, and press. Add

a 2½-inch beige square to these units, as shown at right, and press. Make 40 of these units.

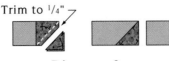

Trim to ¼"

Diagram 8

3 Sew the Step 2 units to both sides of the Step 1 units, as shown in **Diagram 9,** and press. Make a total of 20 Star Blocks. At this point, the Star Blocks should measure 6½ inches square.

Diagram 9

4 Stitch four Star Blocks together, as shown in **Diagram 10,** and press. At this point, these star units should measure 12½ inches square. Make a total of four star units, as shown. Set aside the four remaining Star Blocks for the corner squares in the pieced inner border.

Diagram 10

5 Referring to the **Quilt Diagram** on page 63, sew the House and Star Blocks together

in rows. Press the seam allowances toward the House Blocks. Sew the rows together, as shown, and press.

BORDERS

The yardage given allows for the border strips to be cut on the crosswise grain. The border strips are longer than necessary and will be trimmed later.

Cutting

From the chestnut print fabric:

✦ Cut four 2½ × 44-inch strips for the pieced inner border

From the red print fabric:

✦ Cut four 2½ × 44-inch strips for the pieced inner border

From the green floral fabric:

✦ Cut four 2½ × 44-inch strips for the pieced inner border

✦ Cut six 3½ × 44-inch strips for the outer border

Attaching the Borders

1 Referring to the **Quilt Diagram** on page 63, sew together one chestnut, one red, and one green 2½ × 44-inch strip for each of the four pieced inner border strips, and press.

2 To attach the top and bottom pieced inner border strips, refer to the **Quilt Diagram** for color placement, and page 198 for "Border Instructions."

3 To attach the side pieced inner border strips and Star Blocks, refer to the **Quilt Dia-**

Quilt Diagram

gram, and page 200 for "Borders with Corner Squares."

4 To attach the 3½-inch-wide green floral outer border strips, refer to page 198 for "Border Instructions."

PUTTING IT ALL TOGETHER

1 Cut the 3⅓-yard length of backing fabric in half crosswise to make two 1⅔-yard lengths. Remove the selvages and sew the long edges together. Press the seam allowances open. Trim the backing and batting so they are about 4 inches larger than the quilt top.

2 For quilting ideas, see the **Quilting Design Diagram.** See page 201 for detailed marking, layering, and finishing instructions.

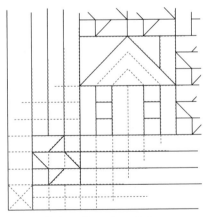

Quilting Design Diagram

BINDING

The 2¾-inch binding strips will produce a ½-inch-wide finished binding. If you want a wider or narrower binding, adjust the width of the strips you cut. (See page 201 for pointers on how to experiment with binding width.) Refer to "Attaching Binding with Mitered Corners" on page 202 to complete your quilt.

Cutting Crosswise Strips

From the green floral binding fabric:

✦ Cut six 2¾ × 44-inch strips on the crosswise grain

HOUSE DRESSING
Framed Block

FABRICS AND SUPPLIES

- One House Block from Welcome Home, page 61
- Four 4½ × 12½-inch border strips in assorted print fabrics
- Four 4½-inch black print fabric corner squares
- Star appliqué shape from My Favorite Things, page 36
- ¼ yard paper-backed fusible web
- Eleven 3-inch squares in assorted print fabrics for star appliqués
- One spool #8 DMC black pearl cotton
- 24-inch square each, of batting and backing
- ⅜ yard plaid fabric for bias binding

1 Sew two of the border strips to the top and bottom of the House Block, as shown in **Diagram 1.** Add corner squares to the remaining two border strips, and sew them to the House Block, referring to the diagram.

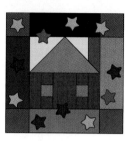

Diagram 1

2 Trace 11 star shapes from page 36 onto the paper side of the fusible web. Following the manufacturer's directions, apply the fusible web to the wrong side of the star fabrics, and cut out the star shapes. Peel off the paper backing.

3 Fuse the stars to the quilt top. Using one strand of pearl cotton, buttonhole stitch the stars in place. Layer the backing, batting, and quilt top. Quilt as desired, and bind with 2¾-inch-wide bias strips.

4 Take the completed House Block to a professional framer for mounting and framing.

Sandy Lavin
Pharmacist

My Life When I'm Not Quilting

Life as a hospital pharmacist in a small-town community hospital/nursing home offers challenge and responsibility. Pharmacy is a fascinating field, filled with new information and the potential for being of real service to people.

Why I Quilt

Quilting is all "mine"—I enjoy spending time creating something of value entirely by myself. It's part of my nature to enjoy meeting a challenge, and every new quilt I make contains interesting ones. I make a lot of quilts as keepsakes for special people, and also for decorating my home.

My Most Memorable Project

The Northwoodsy-Lodge type Christmas tree skirt I recently made for my son and daughter-in-law has been my best-ever quilting experience. I'm happy with everything from my choice of fabrics and positioning of the blocks, to the appliquéd motifs and the buttonhole stitching that surrounds them. I used warm colors from the Thimbleberries palette, which made it an instant favorite with everyone in my family.

My Best Tip for Finding More Time for Quilting

Keep several projects going at the same time—all in different stages of completion. That way, you can keep yourself from getting bored. I like to lay out fabric and a pattern ready to cut in my sewing room, keep something else by my sewing machine waiting to be pieced, and store handwork by my chair in our family room.

> *I think life is what you make it. I function best when I'm overcommitted—and still find time to make quilts.*
>
> —Sandy Lavin

CLIMBING VINES

SIZE

Wall Quilt: 69 inches square (unquilted)
Finished Block: 12 inches square

 ## HOUSE DRESSING

See the Pillow with Ties on the chair.
Directions are given on page 74.

FABRICS AND SUPPLIES

Yardage is based on 44-inch-wide fabric.

+ 1¼ yards floral print fabric for Pieced Blocks

+ 2¼ yards beige print fabric for Pieced Blocks

+ 1 yard purple print fabric for inner border and flower appliqués

+ 2 yards gold print fabric for outer border

+ ⅜ yard rose print fabric for flower center appliqués

+ 1 yard light green print fabric for leaf appliqués

+ 1 yard dark green print fabric for vine appliqués

+ 2 yards freezer paper for appliqué templates

+ ¾ yard gold print fabric for binding

+ 4 yards fabric for quilt backing

+ Quilt batting, at least 73 inches square

+ Rotary cutter, mat, and wide see-through ruler with ⅛-inch markings

+ Removable fabric marker or quilter's silver pencil

Color Play

See page 68 for a creative color variation on the quilt shown here.

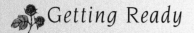

Getting Ready

* Read instructions thoroughly before you begin.

* Note that the appliqué in this project is done using the freezer paper appliqué method. For more information on this type of hand appliqué, see page 70.

* Prewash and press fabric.

* Place right sides of fabric pieces together and use ¼-inch seam allowances throughout unless directions specify otherwise.

* Seam allowances are included in the cutting sizes given.

* Press seam allowances in the direction that will create the least bulk, and whenever possible, press toward the darker fabric. Press border seam allowances toward the borders unless directions specify otherwise.

* Cutting directions for each section of the quilt are given individually. If you like to cut as you go, simply follow the directions as you get to them. If you'd rather cut all your pieces at the same time, skip ahead to find each of the cutting sections and do all the cutting before you begin.

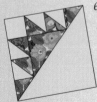

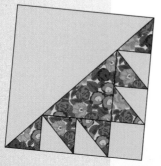

FABRIC KEY
(for the quilt shown on page 67)

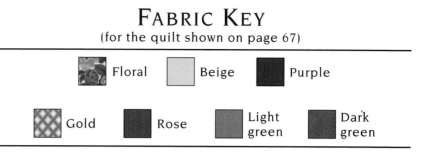

- Floral
- Beige
- Purple
- Gold
- Rose
- Light green
- Dark green

Color Play

The soft floral fabric in the Pieced Blocks of Climbing Vines becomes the main focal print in this colorful variation. A dark green print makes the pieced sections of each block stand out more than in the original quilt, and the absence of flowers, vines, and leaves makes this version of Climbing Vines much speedier to make than its appliquéd cousin.

PIECED BLOCKS

(Make 16)

Cutting

From the floral print fabric:

◆ Cut two $6\frac{7}{8}$ × 44-inch strips. From these strips, cut eight $6\frac{7}{8}$-inch squares.

◆ Cut two $3\frac{7}{8}$ × 44-inch strips. From these strips, cut sixteen $3\frac{7}{8}$-inch squares. Cut these squares in half diagonally to form 32 triangles.

◆ Cut three more $3\frac{7}{8}$ × 44-inch strips for Step 1, below.

From the beige print fabric:

◆ Cut three $12\frac{7}{8}$ × 44-inch strips. From these strips, cut eight $12\frac{7}{8}$-inch squares.

◆ Cut three $3\frac{7}{8}$ × 44-inch strips

◆ Cut two $3\frac{1}{2}$ × 44-inch strips. From these strips, cut sixteen $3\frac{1}{2}$-inch squares.

Piecing

1 Layer three $3\frac{7}{8}$ × 44-inch floral strips and three $3\frac{7}{8}$ × 44-inch beige strips together in pairs, as shown in **Diagram 1,** and press. Cut the layered strips into thirty-two $3\frac{7}{8}$-inch squares, as shown, taking care not to shift the layers as you cut.

$3\frac{7}{8}$"

Diagram 1

2 Cut the layered squares in half diagonally, as shown in **Diagram 2.** Stitch $\frac{1}{4}$ inch from the diagonal edges, as shown, and press. At this point, the 64 triangle-pieced squares should measure $3\frac{1}{2}$ inches square.

Diagram 2

3 Referring to **Diagram 3** for color placement, sew the triangle-pieced squares together in pairs, and press. Make a total of 16 of Unit A and 16 of Unit B, as shown.

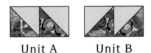

Unit A   Unit B

Diagram 3

4 Cut the $6\frac{7}{8}$-inch floral squares in half diagonally to form 16 triangles. Sew the A units to the top of these floral triangles, as shown in **Diagram 4,** and press.

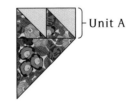

Unit A

Diagram 4

5 Sew the $3\frac{1}{2}$-inch beige squares to the B units, as shown in **Diagram 5.** Press the seam allowances toward the beige squares.

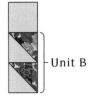

Unit B

Diagram 5

6 Sew the Step 5 units to the left side of the triangle units from Step 4, as shown in **Diagram 6,** and press. Stitch the $3\frac{7}{8}$-inch floral triangles to the ends of the A and B units, as shown, and press.

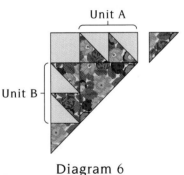

Unit A

Unit B

Diagram 6

7 Cut the $12\frac{7}{8}$-inch beige squares in half diagonally to form 16 triangles. Sew these triangles to the Step 6 units, as shown in **Diagram 7,** and press. Make a total of 16 Pieced Blocks. At this point, the Pieced Blocks should measure $12\frac{1}{2}$ inches square.

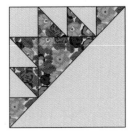

Diagram 7

8 Sew four of the Pieced Blocks together to form the center of the quilt, as shown in **Diagram 8,** and press. Using a removable fabric marker or quilter's silver pencil, draw an 11-inch circle very lightly over the center of these blocks, as shown, as a placement guide for the center vine.

Diagram 8

QUILT CENTER

Cutting

From the dark green fabric:
✦ Cut enough 1⅜-inch-wide bias strips to make a 45-inch-long strip for the center vine

Appliquéing the Center Vine

1 Join two dark green bias strips, right sides together, using a ¼-inch seam allowance, as shown at left in **Diagram 9.** Start and stop exactly at the V-notches of the two strips, and press the seam open, as shown at right. Continue adding bias

strips as needed to complete the center vine.

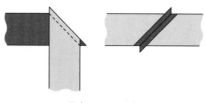

Diagram 9

2 Fold the dark green bias strip in half lengthwise, with wrong sides together, as shown at left in **Diagram 10,** and press. Stitch a scant ¼ inch in from the raw edges, to keep them aligned. Fold the strip in half again, so that the raw edges are hidden by the first folded edge, as shown at right, and press.

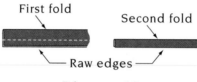
First fold · Second fold · Raw edges

Diagram 10

3 Referring to **Diagram 11,** position the bias strip over the drawn circle in the middle of the quilt. Pin and baste the vine in place. Using matching thread, appliqué the vine to the quilt center, tucking the ends under and stitching them in place, because they will not be covered by other appliqué pieces.

Diagram 11

Appliquéing the Center Leaves

With this method of hand appliqué, the freezer paper forms a base around which each leaf is shaped.

1 Lay a piece of freezer paper, noncoated side up, over the C Leaf shape on page 73, and use a pencil to trace this shape 12 times. Cut out the leaves on your traced lines.

2 With a dry iron on the wool setting, press the coated side of each freezer-paper C Leaf onto the wrong side of the light green leaf fabric. Allow at least ½ inch between each shape for seam allowances.

3 Cut out each C Leaf a scant ¼ inch beyond the edge of the freezer-paper pattern and finger press the seam allowance over the edge of the freezer paper.

4 Referring to **Diagram 12,** position and stitch four clusters of leaves along the center vine with a blind stitch. When there is about ½ inch left to appliqué on each leaf, slide your needle into this opening and loosen the freezer paper. Gently remove it, and finish stitching each leaf in place.

Diagram 12

Assembly

1 Sew eight of the Pieced Blocks together into four pairs, as shown in **Diagram 13,** and press.

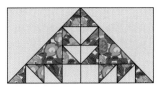

Diagram 13

2 Sew a pair of blocks from Step 1 to the top and bottom of the quilt center, referring to the **Quilt Diagram,** and press.

3 Sew a Pieced Block to each end of the two remaining stitched pairs of Pieced Blocks, as shown in **Diagram 14,** and press. Sew these sections to the sides of the quilt center, referring to the **Quilt Diagram,** and press.

Quilt Diagram

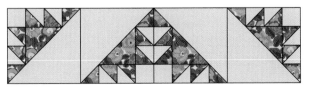

Diagram 14

INNER BORDER

The yardage given allows for the border strips to be cut on the crosswise grain. The border strips are longer than necessary and will be trimmed later.

Cutting

From the purple print fabric:
✦ Cut five 1½ × 44-inch strips for the inner border

Attaching the Inner Border

Adding the inner border helps to stabilize the edges of the quilt before appliquéing the shapes to the quilt center corners.

To attach the 1½-inch-wide purple inner border strips, as shown in the **Quilt Diagram,** refer to page 198 for "Border Instructions."

APPLIQUÉING THE QUILT CENTER CORNERS

Cutting

From the dark green fabric:
✦ Cut enough 1⅜-inch-wide bias strips to make four 50-inch-long strips for the corner vines

Appliquéing the Corner Vines

1 Referring to **Diagram 10** on page 70, fold the 50-inch dark green bias strips in half lengthwise, with wrong sides together, and press. Stitch a scant ¼ inch in from the raw edges, to keep them aligned. Fold the strips in half again, so that the raw edges are hidden by the first folded edge, and press.

2 Position the bias vines on the beige fabric, referring to the **Quilt Diagram** on page 71, making sure that the center circles are 6 inches in diameter, so that the flowers will fit inside them. Pin and baste the corner vines in position. Using matching thread, appliqué the vines to the quilt. The short ends of the vines will be covered by the leaves, so there is no need to stitch them in place.

Appliquéing the Flowers and Leaves

1 Layer a piece of freezer paper, noncoated side up, over A Flower, B Flower Center, and C Leaf on pages 73–74. With a pencil, trace A Flower and B Flower Center 12 times, and C Leaf 84 times, and cut out the shapes on your traced lines.

2 With a dry iron on the wool setting, press the coated side of the freezer-paper shapes onto the wrong side of the fabrics for the flower and leaf appliqués. Allow at least ½ inch between each shape for seam allowances.

3 Cut out each shape a scant ¼ inch beyond the freezer paper edge. Finger press the seam allowances around the edges of the freezer-paper shapes.

4 Referring to the **Quilt Diagram** on page 71, position the flowers, flower centers, and leaves on the quilt top. Using matching thread, appliqué the shapes in place. When there is about ½ inch left to appliqué, remove the freezer paper in the same manner as for the center leaves.

OUTER BORDER

Cutting

From the gold print fabric:
✦ Cut seven 9½ × 44-inch strips

From the dark green print fabric:
✦ Cut enough 1⅜-inch-wide bias strips to make a 330-inch-long strip for the outer border vines

Attaching the Outer Border

To attach the 9½-inch-wide gold outer border strips, as shown in the **Quilt Diagram** on page 71, refer to page 198 for "Border Instructions."

After adding the borders to Climbing Vines, prepare the vines for appliqué and baste them on your quilt with white thread. Pack the quilt in a tote bag or suitcase, along with some needles and thread that matches the fabric in your vines, and you'll have some hand appliqué on hand for times when you are traveling.

Appliquéing the Outer Border

Appliqué the vines, flowers, and leaves to the outer border in the same manner as for the quilt center and corners, referring to the **Quilt Diagram** on page 71 for placement of the appliqués.

PUTTING IT ALL TOGETHER

1 Cut the 4-yard length of backing fabric in half crosswise to make two 2-yard lengths. Remove the selvages and sew the long edges together. Press the seam allowances open. Trim the backing and batting so they are about 4 inches larger than the quilt top.

2 For quilting ideas, see the **Quilting Design Diagram.** See page 201 for detailed marking, layering, and finishing instructions.

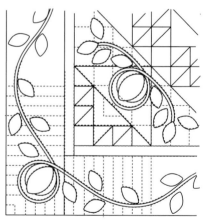

Quilting Design Diagram

BINDING

The 2¾-inch binding strips will produce a ½-inch-wide finished binding. If you want a wider or narrower binding, adjust the width of the strips you cut. (See page 201 for pointers on how to experiment with binding width.) Refer to "Attaching Binding with Mitered Corners" on page 202 to complete your quilt.

Cutting Crosswise Strips

From the gold print binding fabric:

✦ Cut seven 2¾ × 44-inch strips on the crosswise grain

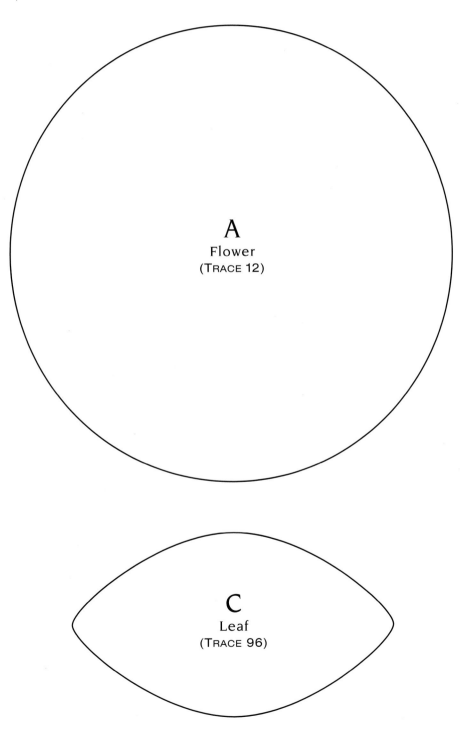

A
Flower
(Trace 12)

C
Leaf
(Trace 96)

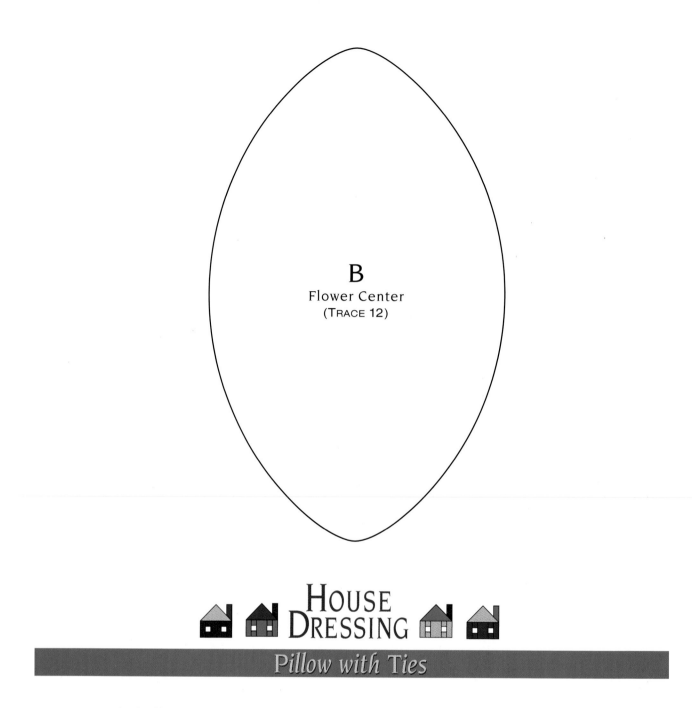

B
Flower Center
(TRACE 12)

HOUSE DRESSING

Pillow with Ties

Finished Pillow: 18 inches square

FABRICS AND SUPPLIES

- ⅔ yard fabric for inner pillowcase
- 1 yard fabric for outer pillowcase
- 18-inch square pillow form

Cutting

From the inner pillowcase fabric:
- Cut one 20½ × 36½-inch rectangle

From the outer pillowcase fabric:
- Cut one 20½ × 36½-inch rectangle
- Cut six 3 × 18½-inch strips for ties

Assembling the Inner Pillowcase

1 To make the hem on the inner pillowcase fabric, turn under 1 inch along the 36½-inch-long edge, referring to **Diagram 1,** and press. Turn under 1 inch again, and press. Edge stitch, as shown in the diagram, using a thread to match the fabric.

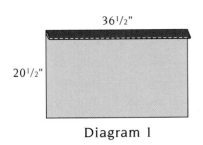

Diagram 1

2 Fold the fabric in half, right sides together, as shown in **Diagram 2.** Stitch a ¼-inch seam along the raw edges, as shown, and turn the pillowcase right side out. Insert the pillow form, and slip stitch the opening closed.

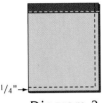

¼"→

Diagram 2

Assembling the Outer Pillowcase

1 Referring to **Diagram 1,** hem the 20½ × 36½-inch rectangle of outer pillowcase fabric in the same manner as for the inner pillowcase.

2 Repeat Step 2 above, as for the inner pillowcase, but do not insert the pillow form or slip stitch the opening closed.

3 To make each of the ties, fold one short end of a 3 × 18½-inch strip under ¼ inch, and press. Fold the long edges of the strip in to meet at the center, as shown in **Diagram 3.**

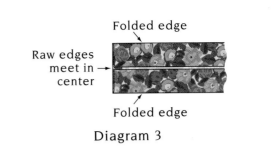

Folded edge

Raw edges meet in center →

Folded edge

Diagram 3

4 Fold the strip in half lengthwise once more, and stitch ⅛ inch away from the folded edges, as shown in **Diagram 4.** Make a total of six of these ¾ × 18½-inch ties.

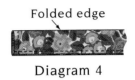

Folded edge

Diagram 4

5 On each side of the opening of the outer pillowcase, insert the raw edges of three ties 1¼ inches to the inside, taking care to space them evenly, as shown in **Diagram 5.** Stitch the ties in place along the edge of the pillowcase, and also through the stitching of the hem, as shown.

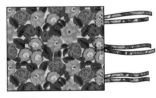

Diagram 5

6 Insert the inner pillow into the outer pillowcase, and tie each of the ties in an overhand decorative knot to finish the pillow.

BACHELOR QUARTERS

SIZE

Bed Quilt: 93 × 123 inches (unquilted)
Finished Blocks: 12 inches square

 ## HOUSE DRESSING

See the Flannel-Backed Blanket on the chair beside the bed.
Directions are given on page 82.

FABRICS AND SUPPLIES

Yardage is based on 44-inch-wide fabric.

+ 3½ yards gold plaid fabric for Blocks A and B

+ 2⅝ yards blue print fabric for Blocks A and B and inner border

+ ⅞ yard gold solid fabric for Block B and lattice posts

+ 3 yards red plaid fabric for lattice pieces

+ 3⅜ yards brown plaid fabric for outer border

+ 1 yard blue print fabric for binding

+ 8¼ yards fabric for quilt backing

+ Quilt batting, at least 97 × 127 inches

+ Rotary cutter, mat, and wide see-through ruler with ⅛-inch markings

Color Play

See page 78 for a creative color variation
on the quilt shown here.

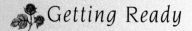 ## Getting Ready

- Read instructions thoroughly before you begin.

- Prewash and press fabric.

- Place right sides of fabric pieces together and use ¼-inch seam allowances throughout unless directions specify otherwise.

- Seam allowances are included in the cutting sizes given.

- Press seam allowances in the direction that will create the least bulk, and whenever possible, press toward the darker fabric. Press border seam allowances toward the borders unless directions specify otherwise.

- Cutting directions for each section of the quilt are given individually. If you like to cut as you go, simply follow the directions as you get to them. If you'd rather cut all your pieces at the same time, skip ahead to find each of the cutting sections and do all the cutting before you begin.

Color Play

For this version of Bachelor Quarters, I chose a very light shade of beige to make the red bars in the pieced blocks stand out visually. And a large-scale blue and red floral print in the border lends a softer, more feminine touch than the more masculine-looking plaid in the project quilt on page 77.

BLOCK A

(Make 17)

Cutting

From the gold plaid fabric:
- Cut eighteen 3½ × 44-inch strips

From the blue print fabric:
- Cut twelve 2 × 44-inch strips

Piecing

Sew together three 3½-inch-wide gold plaid strips and two 2-inch-wide blue strips, as shown in **Diagram 1,** and press. Make six of Strip Set I and cross cut them into seventeen 12½-inch segments, as shown. Make a total of 17 of Block A. At this point, Block A should measure 12½ inches square.

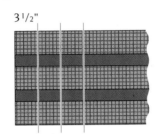

12½"

Strip Set I   Block A
Diagram 1

BLOCK B

(Make 18)

Cutting

From the gold plaid fabric:
- Cut fifteen 3½ × 44-inch strips

From the blue print fabric:
- Cut ten 2 × 44-inch strips

- Cut six 3½ × 44-inch strips

From the gold solid fabric:
- Cut four 2 × 44-inch strips

Piecing

1 Sew together three 3½-inch-wide gold plaid strips and two 2-inch-wide blue strips together, as shown in **Diagram 2,** and press. Make five of Strip Set II, and cross cut them into a total of fifty-four 3½-inch segments, as shown in the diagram.

3½"

Strip Set II
Diagram 2

2 Sew three 3½-inch-wide blue strips and two 2-inch-wide gold solid strips together, as shown in **Diagram 3,** and press. Make two of Strip Set III, and cross cut them into a total of thirty-six 2-inch segments, as shown in the diagram.

2"

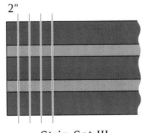

Strip Set III
Diagram 3

3 Sew three Strip Set II segments and two Strip Set III segments together to make Block B, as shown in **Diagram 4,** and press. Make a total of 18 of Block B. At this point, Block B should measure 12½ inches square.

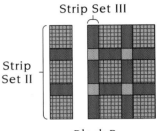

Strip Set III

Strip Set II

Block B
Diagram 4

QUILT CENTER

Cutting

From the red plaid fabric:
- Cut twenty-eight 3½ × 44-inch strips. From these strips, cut eighty-two 3½ × 12½-inch lattice pieces.

From the gold solid fabric:
- Cut four 3½ × 44-inch strips. From these strips, cut forty-eight 3½-inch squares for lattice posts.

Piecing

1 Sew five 3½ × 12½-inch red lattice pieces and six 3½-inch square gold lattice posts together, as shown in **Diagram 5,** and press. Make eight horizontal lattice strips.

Diagram 5

2 Referring to the **Quilt Diagram** for block placement, sew Blocks A and B, and the 3½ × 12½-inch red lattice pieces together to form seven horizontal rows. Three of the seven rows will start and end with A Blocks, and four rows will start and end with B Blocks. Sew a 3½ × 12½-inch red lattice piece to both ends of each row, and press.

3 Referring to the **Quilt Diagram,** sew the seven horizontal rows and eight lattice strips together, and press.

Quilt Diagram

BORDERS

The yardage given allows for the inner border strips to be cut on the crosswise grain and the outer border strips to be cut on the lengthwise grain. The border strips are longer than necessary and will be trimmed later.

Cutting

From the blue print fabric:

✦ Cut ten 2 × 44-inch strips for the inner border

From the brown plaid fabric, on the lengthwise grain:

✦ Cut two 6½ × 86-inch strips for the top and bottom outer border

✦ Cut two 6½ × 127-inch strips for the side outer border

Attaching the Borders

1 To attach the 2-inch-wide blue inner border strips, as shown in the **Quilt Diagram,** refer to page 198 for "Border Instructions."

2 To attach the 6½-inch-wide brown plaid outer border strips, as shown in the **Quilt Diagram,** refer to page 198 for "Border Instructions."

PUTTING IT ALL TOGETHER

1 Cut the 8¼-yard length of backing fabric in thirds crosswise to make three 2¾-yard lengths. Remove the selvages and sew the long edges together. Press the seam allowances open. Trim the backing and batting so they are about 4 inches larger than the quilt top.

2 For quilting ideas, see the **Quilting Design Diagram.**

See page 201 for detailed marking, layering, and finishing instructions.

Quilting Design Diagram

BINDING

The 2¾-inch binding strips will produce a ½-inch-wide finished binding. If you want a wider or narrower binding, adjust the width of the strips you cut. (See page 201 for pointers on how to experiment with binding width.) Refer to "Attaching Binding with Mitered Corners" on page 202 to complete your quilt.

Cutting Crosswise Strips

From the blue print binding fabric:
+ Cut eleven 2¾ × 44-inch strips on the crosswise grain

ROAD TRIP *Taking hand quilting on the road can be easier than you might think at first— even if you're working on a bed-size quilt. To carry a large quilt comfortably and safely when traveling, fold the quilt so that half of it will slip into a queen- or king-size pillowcase. Then cover up the other end with another pillowcase of the same size, and use several rust-proof, brass safety pins to pin the pillowcases together where they overlap. (Take care not to catch the quilt in the pins when doing this.) Gather up the other supplies needed for hand quilting, including your preferred size hoop, a few packages of your favorite brand and size of quilting needles, at least two thimbles that fit you well (in case one somehow misplaces itself), thread, small scissors or thread snips, some rolls of masking tape or painter's tape in various widths for quilting evenly spaced grid lines, and a couple of needle threaders. Tuck these items into another pillowcase, and tie a simple overhand knot at the top. Everything will stay protected, be easy to pack in a car or a suitcase, and be accessible whenever you want to stitch.*

FABRICS AND SUPPLIES

+ Purchased wool blanket

+ Pieced flannel backing, 4 inches larger on all sides than wool blanket

1 Lay the flannel backing on a flat surface, with the wrong side up. Center the wool blanket on top, with the right side facing up, so that 4 inches of flannel are showing on all sides.

2 Baste the two layers together, and machine quilt as desired.

3 To form the binding, fold the 4-inch width of flannel in on one side of the blanket, so that the raw edge of the flannel is aligned with the edge of the blanket, as shown in **Diagram 1.** Fold the flannel in once more, so that it overlaps the blanket by 2 inches, as shown at right in the diagram. Hand stitch the folded edge of the flannel binding to the blanket.

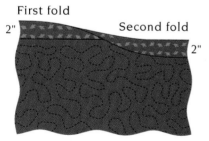

Diagram 1

4 Continue hand stitching the flannel binding in place all the way to the edge of the blanket, as shown in **Diagram 2.**

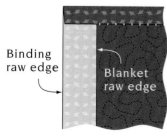

Diagram 2

5 At the corner, fold the corner of the flannel down at a 45-degree angle, as shown in **Diagram 3.**

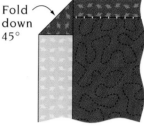

Diagram 3

6 Fold the flannel in to meet the raw edge of the blanket on this side, as shown at the top of **Diagram 4.** Fold the flannel in again, as in Step 3, so that it overlaps the blanket by 2 inches. Hand stitch the mitered corner in place on this side of the blanket, as shown at the bottom of the diagram, and continue stitching to the next corner. Repeat the mitering process at each corner of the blanket.

Diagram 4

Suzanne Nelson
Managing Editor of Rodale Quilt Books

My Life When I'm Not Quilting

I have a job that is a quilter's idea of heaven. As the Managing Editor of Rodale Quilt Books, I get to think about, write about, and pore over photos of quilts all day long.

Why I Quilt

The minute I took my first quilting class, I knew I had found my place in the universe. Everything about quilt-making is deeply satisfying to me. I juggle a demanding job with being a wife and mother of two girls, and running a household. The only way I keep everything in balance is by making it a point to do some form of quilt-making every day.

My Most Memorable Project

I finished the very first bed-size quilt I made for my daughter Emmy early one morning at 1:00 A.M. I tiptoed up the stairs and gently put the quilt over her while she lay sleeping. When she woke up, she was enchanted that her quilt had magically shown up in the middle of the night. I've also surprised Emmy's sister, Liana, with a similar visit by the "quilt fairy"—it is satisfying beyond words.

My Best Tip for Finding More Time for Quilting

The best thing I did for both timesaving and efficiency was to go to a home supply store and buy a stock kitchen cabinet. It is the perfect height for rotary cutting, and a large-size cutting mat fits comfortably on top. I keep my rulers and rotary cutters in the drawers and fabrics for projects in the cabinets underneath.

I've given up on having the perfect house, in spotless condition at all times. I want my daughters to remember me sitting at my sewing machine, with a smile on my face, instead of fussing over dust particles. Making quilts is a tangible way for me to wrap them up in my love.

—Suzanne Nelson

BEDTIME STORY

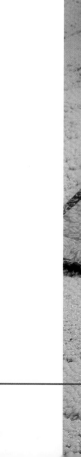

SIZE

Crib Quilt: 44 × 54 inches (unquilted)
Finished Block: 8 inches square

FABRICS AND SUPPLIES

Yardage is based on 44-inch-wide fabric.

- 2⅛ yards beige print fabric for Pieced Blocks and inner border

- 1¼ yards gold print fabric for Pieced Blocks, lattice posts, and outer border

- ⅞ yard red print fabric for lattice pieces and inner border corners

- ⅝ yard red print fabric for binding

- 2⅔ yards fabric for quilt backing

- Quilt batting, at least 48 × 58 inches

- Rotary cutter, mat, and wide see-through ruler with ⅛-inch markings

Color Play

See page 86 for a creative color variation on the quilt shown here.

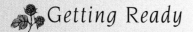 Getting Ready

- Read instructions thoroughly before you begin.

- Prewash and press fabric.

- Place right sides of fabric pieces together and use ¼-inch seam allowances throughout unless directions specify otherwise.

- Seam allowances are included in the cutting sizes given.

- Press seam allowances in the direction that will create the least bulk, and whenever possible, press toward the darker fabric. Press border seam allowances toward the borders unless directions specify otherwise.

- Cutting directions for each section of the quilt are given individually. If you like to cut as you go, simply follow the directions as you get to them. If you'd rather cut all your pieces at the same time, skip ahead to find each of the cutting sections and do all the cutting before you begin.

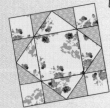

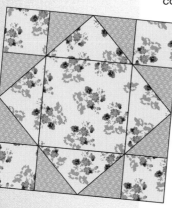

FABRIC KEY
(for the quilt shown on page 85)

Beige	Gold	Red

Color Play

For this color variation, I wanted to create a brighter, clearer color combination than in the soft, criblike Bedtime Story quilt on page 85. Green lattices and a striking, large-scale floral print produce a more sophisticated color combination with a French country look.

PIECED BLOCKS

(Make 12)

Cutting

From the beige print fabric:

✦ Cut twelve 4½-inch squares

✦ Cut three 2½ × 44-inch strips. From these strips, cut forty-eight 2½-inch squares.

✦ Cut six more 2½ × 44-inch strips. From these strips, cut forty-eight 2½ × 4½-inch rectangles.

From the gold print fabric:

✦ Cut six 2½ × 44-inch strips. From these strips, cut ninety-six 2½-inch squares.

Piecing

1 Position a 2½-inch gold square on the corner of a 2½ × 4½-inch beige rectangle, as shown at the top of **Diagram 1.** Stitch diagonally from corner to corner on the gold squares, as shown at the top of the diagram. Trim the seam allowance to ¼ inch, and press. Repeat this process at the opposite corner of the beige rectangle, as shown at the bottom of the diagram. Make a total of 48 of these units.

Trim to ¹/₄"

Trim to ¹/₄"

Diagram 1

2 Sew a Step 1 unit to the top and bottom of the twelve 4½-inch beige squares, as shown in **Diagram 2.**

Diagram 2

3 Sew 2½-inch beige squares to both sides of the remaining Step 1 units, as shown in **Diagram 3,** and press.

Diagram 3

4 Referring to **Diagram 4,** sew the Step 3 units to both sides of the Step 2 units and press. Make a total of 12 Pieced Blocks. At this point, the Pieced Blocks should measure 8½ inches square.

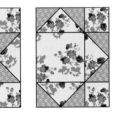

Diagram 4

QUILT CENTER

Cutting

From the red print fabric:

✦ Cut eight 2½ × 44-inch strips. From these strips, cut thirty-one 2½ × 8½-inch lattice pieces.

From the gold print fabric:

✦ Cut two 2½ × 44-inch strips. From these strips, cut twenty 2½-inch square lattice posts.

Piecing

1 Sew three 2½ × 8½-inch red lattice pieces and four 2½-inch square gold lattice posts together for each lattice strip, as shown in **Diagram 5,** and press. Make a total of five of these lattice strips.

2 Sew three Pieced Blocks and four 2½ × 8½-inch red lattice pieces together, as shown in **Diagram 6,** and press. Make a total of four of these block rows.

3 Referring to the **Quilt Diagram** on page 88, sew the block rows and lattice strips together to form the quilt center, and press.

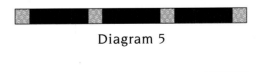

Diagram 5

Diagram 6

Quilt Diagram

BORDERS

The yardage given allows for the border strips to be cut on the crosswise grain. The border strips are longer than necessary and will be trimmed later.

Cutting

From the beige print fabric:

✦ Cut four 4½ × 44-inch strips. From these strips, cut two 4½ × 28½-inch strips, two 4½ × 38½-inch strips, and four 4½-inch corner squares.

From the red print fabric:

✦ Cut one 2½ × 44-inch strip. From this strip, cut eight 2½ × 4½-inch rectangles for the inner border corners.

From the gold print fabric:

✦ Cut five 2½ × 44-inch strips for the outer border

Assembly

1 Referring to the **Quilt Diagram,** sew a 2½ × 4½-inch red rectangle to each end of the two 4½ × 28½-inch beige strips, and press. Sew these border strips to the top and bottom of the quilt, and press.

2 Referring to the **Quilt Diagram,** sew a 2½ × 4½-inch red rectangle to each end of the two 4½ × 38½-inch beige strips, and press. Sew the 4½-inch beige squares to the ends of these border strips, and press. Sew the border strips to the sides of the quilt, and press.

3 To attach the 2½-inch-wide gold outer border strips, as shown in the **Quilt Diagram,** refer to page 198 for "Border Instructions."

PUTTING IT ALL TOGETHER

1 Cut the 2⅔-yard length of backing fabric in half crosswise to make two 1⅓-yard lengths. Remove the selvages and sew the long edges together. Press the seam allowances open. Trim the backing and batting so they are about 4 inches larger than the quilt top.

Plan Ahead

Cut a 4½-inch-wide strip of backing fabric to use as a hanging sleeve. It is nice to have the sleeve match the quilt back and ready to attach if you decide you want to display Bedtime Story as a wall quilt.

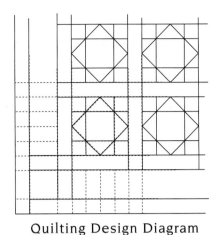

Quilting Design Diagram

2 For quilting ideas, see the **Quilting Design Diagram.** See page 201 for detailed marking, layering, and finishing instructions.

BINDING

The 2¾-inch binding strips will produce a ½-inch-wide finished binding. If you want a wider or narrower binding, adjust the width of the strips you cut. (See page 201 for pointers on how to experiment with binding width.) Refer to "Attaching Binding with Mitered Corners" on page 202 to complete your quilt.

Cutting Crosswise Strips

From the red print binding fabric:
- ✦ Cut five 2¾ × 44-inch strips on the crosswise grain

At times, your finished quilt may end up traveling without you. If you make a baby quilt like Bedtime Story as a gift for a friend, it's nice to know that sending it through the mail can be both simple and safe, just by following a few helpful guidelines. First, fold the quilt carefully and place it in a thick plastic bag to keep it safe from moisture and dirt in case the shipping box splits open. Inside the bag, include a large index card or piece of paper that clearly states your name and address, as well as the name and address of the person you're sending it to. After closing the top of the bag securely with a piece of packing tape or a strong twist tie, place the bag into a cardboard box and place **another label inside the box**, containing the same address information. Then fill the space around the plastic bag with packing material to cushion and protect the quilt during shipment. Recycled Styrofoam peanuts, plastic bubble wrap, or large pieces of scrunched-up, plain paper are all good, lightweight options that will keep the quilt from becoming wrinkled or moving around inside the box. When choosing a company for shipping your quilt, look for one that will allow you to insure the quilt for its value and can track the progress of your package as it travels.

MY STARS

SIZE

Bed Quilt: 88 × 108 inches (unquilted)
Finished Block: 16 inches square

HOUSE DRESSING

See the Pieced and Ruffled Pillows on the bed.
Directions are given on page 96.

FABRICS AND SUPPLIES

Yardage is based on 44-inch-wide fabric.

+ 2⅞ yards blue print #1 fabric for Star Blocks and middle border

+ 3½ yards red print fabric for Star Blocks, star lattice posts, and outer border

+ 3⅞ yards beige print fabric for Star Blocks, star point border, and inner border

+ 2¼ yards blue print #2 fabric for lattice pieces

+ 1 yard blue print #1 fabric for binding

+ 7⅞ yards fabric for quilt backing

+ Quilt batting, at least 92 × 112 inches

+ Rotary cutter, mat, and wide see-through ruler with ⅛-inch markings

❦ Read instructions thoroughly before you begin.

❦ Prewash and press fabric.

❦ Place right sides of fabric pieces together and use ¼-inch seam allowances throughout unless directions specify otherwise.

❦ Seam allowances are included in the cutting sizes given.

❦ Press seam allowances in the direction that will create the least bulk, and whenever possible, press toward the darker fabric. Press border seam allowances toward the borders unless directions specify otherwise.

❦ Cutting directions for each section of the quilt are given individually. If you like to cut as you go, simply follow the directions as you get to them. If you'd rather cut all your pieces at the same time, skip ahead to find each of the cutting sections and do all the cutting before you begin.

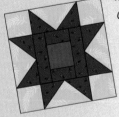

STAR BLOCKS

(Make 12)

Cutting

From the blue print #1 fabric:
◆ Cut four 2½ × 44-inch strips

◆ Cut five more 2½ × 44-inch strips. From these strips, cut twenty-four 2½ × 8½-inch rectangles.

◆ Cut eleven 4½ × 44-inch strips. From these strips, cut ninety-six 4½-inch squares.

From the red print fabric:
◆ Cut two 4½ × 44-inch strips

From the beige print fabric:
◆ Cut twelve 4½ × 44-inch strips. From these strips, cut forty-eight 4½ × 8½-inch rectangles.

◆ Cut six more 4½ × 44-inch strips. From these strips, cut forty-eight 4½-inch squares.

Plan Ahead

My Stars requires lots of 2½- and 4½-inch strips, which are commonly used strip widths for many quilt patterns. Consider cutting a few extra strips in each fabric when you're cutting the strips for this quilt. Save the extra strips and store them in bundles clipped with large office clips. That way, you'll begin to build up a stash of precut strips that will come in handy for Log Cabin quilts or other projects in the future.

Piecing

1 Sew a 2½ × 44-inch blue strip to each side of the two 4½ × 44-inch red strips, as shown in **Diagram 1,** and press. Cross cut these strip sets into twelve 4½-inch-wide segments, as shown.

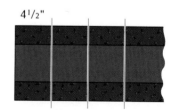

4½"

Diagram 1

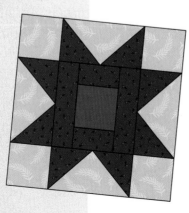

2 Sew the 2½ × 8½-inch blue rectangles to both sides of the Step 1 segments, as shown in **Diagram 2,** and press.

Diagram 2

3 Position a 4½-inch blue square on the corner of a 4½ × 8½-inch beige rectangle, as shown at the top of **Diagram 3.** Stitch diagonally from corner to corner on the blue square. Trim the seam allowance to ¼ inch, and press. Repeat this process at the opposite corner of the beige rectangle, as shown at the bottom of the diagram. Make a total of 48 of these units.

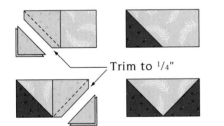

Diagram 3

4 Sew a star point unit to the top and the bottom of each of the Step 2 units, as shown in **Diagram 4,** and press.

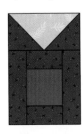

Diagram 4

5 Referring to **Diagram 5,** sew the 4½-inch beige squares to both sides of each of the remaining Step 3 star point units, and press. Sew these units to both sides of the Step 4 units, as shown. Make a total of 12 Star Blocks. At this point, the Star Blocks should measure 16½ inches square.

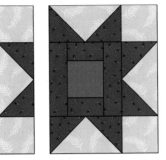

Diagram 5

QUILT CENTER

Cutting

From the red print fabric:
◆ Cut three 4½ × 44-inch strips. From these strips, cut twenty 4½-inch squares for lattice posts.

◆ Cut eight 2½ × 44-inch strips. From these strips, cut one hundred twenty-four 2½-inch squares for star points.

From the blue print #2 fabric:
◆ Cut sixteen 4½ × 44-inch strips. From these strips, cut thirty-one 4½ × 16½-inch lattice pieces.

Piecing

1 Position a 2½-inch red square on each of the upper two corners of a 4½ × 16½-inch blue rectangle, as shown at the top of **Diagram 6.** Stitch diagonally on the red squares. Trim the seam allowances to ¼ inch, as shown, and press. Repeat this process at the lower two corners of each blue rectangle, as shown in the lower part of the diagram. Make a total of 31 of these lattice pieces, as shown at the bottom of the diagram.

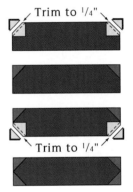

Diagram 6

2 Sew together four lattice pieces and three Star Blocks, as shown in **Diagram 7,** and press. Make a total of four of these block rows.

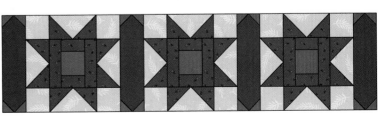

Diagram 7

3 Sew together four 4½-inch square red lattice posts and three lattice pieces, as shown in **Diagram 8,** and press. Make a total of five of these lattice strips.

4 Sew the block rows and lattice strips together to form the quilt center, referring to the **Quilt Diagram,** and press.

BORDERS

The yardage given allows for the border strips to be cut on the crosswise grain. The border strips are longer than necessary and will be trimmed later.

Cutting

From the beige print fabric:
✦ Cut ten 2½ × 44-inch strips for the star point border. From these strips, cut fourteen 2½ × 16½-inch strips, eighteen 2½ × 4½-inch rectangles, and four 2½-inch squares.

✦ Cut eight more 2½ × 44-inch strips for the inner border

From the blue print #1 fabric:
✦ Cut nine 2½ × 44-inch strips for the middle border

From the red print fabric:
✦ Cut three 2½ × 44-inch strips. From these strips, cut thirty-six 2½-inch squares for the star point border

✦ Cut eleven 6½ × 44-inch strips for the outer border

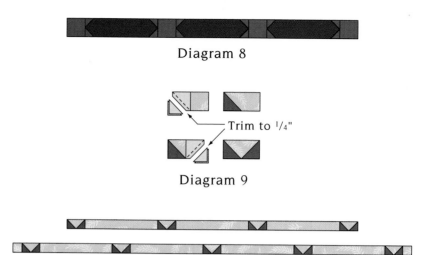

Diagram 8

Trim to ¼"

Diagram 9

Diagram 10

Quilt Diagram

Piecing

1 Position a 2½-inch red square on the corner of a 2½ × 4½-inch beige rectangle, as shown at top left in **Diagram 9** on page 94. Draw a diagonal line on the red square, and stitch on this line. Trim away the excess corner fabric, leaving a ¼-inch seam allowance, and press, as shown at top right. Repeat at the opposite corner of the beige rectangle, creating a star point unit, as shown at lower right. Make a total of 18 of these star point units.

2 Sew four star point units and three 2½ × 16½-inch beige strips together, as shown at the top of **Diagram 10** on page 94, and press. Make two of these border strips, sew them to the top and bottom of the quilt center, referring to the **Quilt Diagram** on page 94, and press.

3 Referring to the lower portion of **Diagram 10,** sew together five star point units, four 2½ × 16½-inch beige strips, and two 2½-inch beige squares, and press. Make two of these border strips, sew them to the sides of the quilt, referring to the **Quilt Diagram,** and press.

4 To attach the 2½-inch-wide beige inner border strips, as shown in the **Quilt Diagram,** refer to page 198 for "Border Instructions."

5 To attach the 2½-inch-wide blue middle border strips, as shown in the **Quilt Diagram,** refer to page 198 for "Border Instructions."

6 To attach the 6½-inch-wide red outer border strips, as shown in the **Quilt Diagram,** refer to page 198 for "Border Instructions."

PUTTING IT ALL TOGETHER

1 Cut the 7⅞-yard length of backing fabric in thirds crosswise to make three 2⅝-yard lengths. Remove the selvages and sew the long edges together. Press the seam allowances open. Trim the backing and batting so they are about 4 inches larger than the quilt top.

2 For quilting ideas, see the **Quilting Design Diagram.** See page 201 for detailed marking, layering, and finishing instructions.

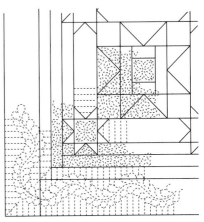

Quilting Design Diagram

BINDING

The 2¾-inch binding strips will produce a ½-inch-wide finished binding. If you want a wider or narrower binding, adjust the width of the strips you cut. (See page 201 for pointers on how to experiment with binding width.) Refer to "Attaching Binding with Mitered Corners" on page 202 to complete your quilt.

Cutting Crosswise Strips

From the blue print #1 binding fabric:

◆ Cut ten 2¾ × 44-inch strips on the crosswise grain

HOUSE DRESSING

Pieced and Ruffled Pillow

Finished Pillow: 18 inches square (without ruffle)

FABRICS AND SUPPLIES
(for 1 pillow)

+ 16-inch Star Block from My Stars, page 92

+ 1⅛ yards red print fabric for border, outer ruffle, and pillow back

+ ⅜ yard blue print fabric for inner ruffle

+ 18-inch square pillow form

Sewing two fabric strips in different widths together creates the illusion of a double ruffle without all the additional bulk.

Cutting

From the red print fabric:
+ Cut two 1½ × 44-inch strips for the border

+ Cut four 3¾ × 44-inch strips for the outer ruffle

From the blue print fabric:
+ Cut four 2½ × 44-inch strips for the inner ruffle

Piecing

1 To make the pillow top, sew 1½-inch-wide red border strips to the top, bottom, and sides of the 16-inch Star Block.

2 Piece the 2½ × 44-inch blue inner ruffle strips together with diagonal seams, referring to page 198 for "Diagonal Piecing." Piece the 3¾ × 44-inch red outer ruffle strips together with diagonal seams.

Sew these strips together along the long edges, with right sides together, as shown in **Diagram 1.**

Diagram 1

3 With right sides facing, sew the short raw edges of the ruffle strip together with a diagonal seam to make a continuous ruffle strip, as shown in **Diagram 2.**

Diagram 2

4 Fold the continuous ruffle strip in half lengthwise, with wrong sides together, and press. Run a line of gathering stitches ¼ inch in from the raw edges, as shown in **Diagram 3.**

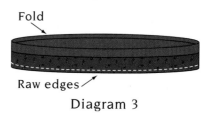

Fold

Raw edges

Diagram 3

5 Position the continuous ruffle strip on the pillow top, with right sides together and raw edges even, as shown in **Diagram 4.** Pull up the gathering stitches, so that the ruffle fits the pillow square. Pin and sew the ruffle to the pillow top, stitching a scant ¼ inch from the raw edges.

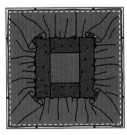

Diagram 4

Cutting

From the red print fabric:
✦ Cut two 18½ × 21-inch pieces for the pillow back

Assembly

1 Fold the two pillow back pieces in half, with wrong sides together, to form two 10½ × 18½-inch double-thick back pieces, as shown in **Diagram 5.** Overlap the two folded edges by 2 inches, as shown, and stitch across the folds, ¼ inch from the edge to secure. The double thickness of each piece will make the pillow back more stable and give it a nice finishing touch.

Overlap 2"

Diagram 5

2 Layer the pillow back and the completed pillow top, with right sides facing. If a ruffle is being added, it will be turned toward the center of the pillow at this time. Pin the front to the back. Stitch together around all the outside edges, using a ¼-inch seam allowance.

3 Trim the corner seam allowances if needed. Turn the pillow right side out, as shown in **Diagram 6,** and fluff up the ruffle. Insert the pillow form through the back opening.

Diagram 6

INDEPENDENCE

SIZE

Wall Quilt: 42 inches square (unquilted)
Finished Blocks: 6 inches square

HOUSE DRESSING

The Place Mats are shown in the basket and on the sideboard.
Directions are given on page 103.

FABRICS AND SUPPLIES

Yardage is based on 44-inch-wide fabric.

+ ¾ yard gold print #1 fabric for outer star appliqués

+ 1 yard gold print #2 fabric for inner star appliqués and inner and outer borders

+ ¾ yard red print fabric for Rail Fence Blocks

+ 1¼ yards blue print fabric for Rail Fence Blocks, star background, and middle border

+ 2 yards paper-backed fusible web

+ One spool #8 DMC black pearl cotton

+ ½ yard red print fabric for binding

+ 1⅜ yards fabric for quilt backing

+ Quilt batting, at least 46 inches square

+ Rotary cutter, mat, and wide see-through ruler with ⅛-inch markings

Color Play

See page 100 for a creative color variation on the quilt shown here.

98

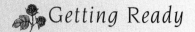 *Getting Ready*

- Read instructions thoroughly before you begin.

- Note that the appliqué in this project is done using the fusible appliqué method.

- Prewash and press fabric.

- Place right sides of fabric pieces together and use ¼-inch seam allowances throughout unless directions specify otherwise.

- Seam allowances are included in the cutting sizes given.

- Press seam allowances in the direction that will create the least bulk, and whenever possible, press toward the darker fabric. Press border seam allowances toward the borders unless directions specify otherwise.

- Cutting directions for each section of the quilt are given individually. If you like to cut as you go, simply follow the directions as you get to them. If you'd rather cut all your pieces at the same time, skip ahead to find each of the cutting sections and do all the cutting before you begin.

FABRIC KEY
(for the quilt shown on page 99)

Gold #1   Gold #2   Red   Blue

Color Play

Medium shades of red, gold, and blue give the Independence quilt on page 99 a soft, casual style that blends comfortably into any decor. For this color variation, I chose deeper shades of red and gold, and added a touch of black to create a more dramatic-looking quilt.

RAIL FENCE BLOCKS

(Make 13)

Cutting

From the red print fabric:
- ◆ Cut six 2½ × 44-inch strips

From the blue print fabric:
- ◆ Cut three 2½ × 44-inch strips

Piecing

Sew a 2½-inch-wide red strip to both sides of each of the 2½-inch-wide blue strips, as shown in **Diagram 1,** and press. Make three of these strip sets, and cross cut them into thirteen 6½-inch segments for the Rail Fence Blocks, as shown.

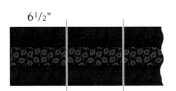

6½"

Diagram 1

STAR BLOCKS

(Make 16)

Cutting

From the blue print fabric:
- ◆ Cut three 6½ × 44-inch strips. From these strips, cut sixteen 6½-inch squares.

Appliquéing

1 Position the fusible web (paper side facing up) over the appliqué shapes on page 102. Trace 16 A Stars and 16 B Stars onto the fusible web, taking care to leave approximately ½ inch between each shape.

2 Roughly cut around the traced lines of the star shapes, as shown in **Diagram 2.**

NOTE: *When you are preparing large shapes like these stars for fusible appliqué, fuse just the outer edges, so that the fabric will not look stiff when finished. To do this, draw a line about ⅜ inch inside each star, and cut away the fusible web on this line, as shown.*

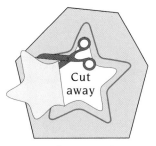

Diagram 2

3 With a hot, dry iron, press the coated side of each fusible web star shape to the wrong side of the gold print fabrics, as shown in **Diagram 3.** Let the fabric cool, and cut out the star shapes directly on your traced outlines. Peel off the paper backing.

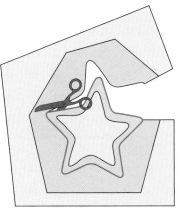

Diagram 3

4 Referring to the **Quilt Diagram,** position the A Star appliqués on the sixteen 6½-inch blue squares, and fuse them in place. Make sure to center each star with the points at least ⅜ inch from the edge of the squares, to allow for seam allowances. Position the B Star appliqués on top of the A Stars, and fuse them in place, as shown.

Quilt Diagram

5 Using the buttonhole stitch and one strand of pearl cotton, appliqué the shapes in place. Refer to page 197 for "Decorative Stitches."

ASSEMBLY

Referring to the **Quilt Diagram** *on page 101 for block placement, sew the Star Blocks and Rail Fence Blocks together in horizontal rows, and press. Sew the rows together to form the quilt center, and press. Set aside the four remaining Star Blocks for the corner squares in the pieced border.*

BORDERS

The yardage given allows for the border strips to be cut on the crosswise grain. The border strips are longer than necessary and will be trimmed later.

Cutting

From the gold print #2 fabric:
+ Cut eight 2½ × 44-inch strips for the inner and outer borders

From the blue print fabric:
+ Cut four 2½ × 44-inch strips for the middle border

Attaching the Borders

1 Sew a 2½ × 44-inch-wide gold strip to both sides of each

of the 2½ × 44-inch blue strips, and press.

2 To attach the top and bottom border units, as shown in the **Quilt Diagram** on page 101, refer to page 198 for "Border Instructions."

3 To attach the side border units with Star Block corner squares, as shown in the **Quilt Diagram,** refer to page 200 for "Borders with Corner Squares."

PUTTING IT ALL TOGETHER

1 Because the size of this quilt is so close to a standard width of fabric, the backing can be made with a 1⅜-yard length of fabric, with no piecing necessary. Trim the backing and batting so they are about 2 inches larger than the quilt top.

2 For quilting ideas, see the **Quilting Design Diagram** on page 103. See page 201 for detailed marking, layering, and finishing instructions.

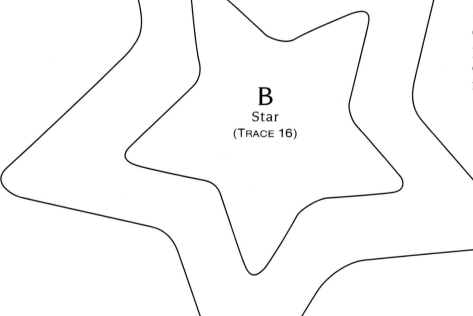

A
Star
(TRACE 16)

B
Star
(TRACE 16)

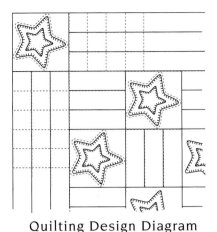

Quilting Design Diagram

BINDING

The 2¾-inch binding strips will produce a ½-inch-wide finished binding. If you want a wider or narrower binding, adjust the width of the strips you cut. (See page 201 for pointers on how to experiment with binding width.) Refer to "Attaching Binding with Mitered Corners" on page 202 to complete your quilt.

Cutting Crosswise Strips

From the red print binding fabric:

✦ Cut five 2¾ × 44-inch strips on the crosswise grain

HOUSE DRESSING

Place Mats

Finished Place Mats: 12 × 18 inches

FABRICS AND SUPPLIES
(for 4 place mats)

✦ ¾ yard blue print fabric for place mats

✦ ¾ yard red print fabric for place mats

✦ ½ yard gold plaid fabric for outer star appliqués

✦ ¼ yard gold print fabric for inner star appliqués

✦ ¾ yard gold print for binding

✦ ½ yard paper-backed fusible web

✦ Star appliqué shapes from page 102

✦ One spool #8 DMC black pearl cotton

Cutting (for *each* place mat)

✦ Cut two 2½ × 44-inch blue strips

✦ Cut one 2½ × 44-inch red strip

✦ Cut two 2¾ × 44-inch binding strips

1 Sew the 2½-inch-wide blue strips to the sides of the 2½-inch-wide red strip, and press. Cross cut the strips into six 6½-inch-wide segments, as shown in **Diagram 1.**

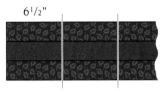

6½"

Diagram 1

2 Sew the segments together to make the place mat, as shown in **Diagram 2.**

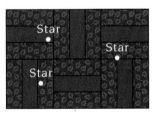

Star Star Star

Diagram 2

3 Trace three A Stars and three B Stars from page 102 onto fusible web. Fuse the stars to the gold plaid and print fabrics. Cut out the stars and fuse them to the place mat, referring to **Diagram 2** for placement.

4 Using one strand of black pearl cotton, buttonhole stitch the stars in place.

5 Quilt the place mat as desired, and bind in the same manner as a quilt.

PATCHES AND PLAIDS

MAKE IT IN A WEEKEND

SIZE

Bed Quilt: 88 × 102 inches (unquilted)
Finished Block: 12 inches square

FABRICS AND SUPPLIES

Yardage is based on 44-inch-wide fabric.

+ 2⅔ yards red print fabric for Nine Patch Blocks and inner border

+ 2½ yards beige print fabric for Nine Patch Blocks and Triangle-Pieced Square Blocks

+ 3⅛ yards red-chestnut-blue plaid fabric for Triangle-Pieced Square Blocks, lattice pieces, and corner squares

+ 2⅓ yards blue print fabric for lattice posts and outer border

+ 1 yard red-chestnut-blue plaid fabric for bias binding

+ 8 yards fabric for quilt backing

+ Quilt batting, at least 92 × 106 inches

+ Rotary cutter, mat, and wide see-through ruler with ⅛-inch markings

Color Play

See page 106 for a creative color variation on the quilt shown here.

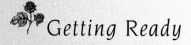

Getting Ready

❧ Read instructions thoroughly before you begin.

❧ Prewash and press fabric.

❧ Place right sides of fabric pieces together and use ¼-inch seam allowances throughout unless directions specify otherwise.

❧ Seam allowances are included in the cutting sizes given.

❧ Press seam allowances in the direction that will create the least bulk, and whenever possible, press toward the darker fabric. Press border seam allowances toward the borders unless directions specify otherwise.

❧ Cutting directions for each section of the quilt are given individually. If you like to cut as you go, simply follow the directions as you get to them. If you'd rather cut all your pieces at the same time, skip ahead to find each of the cutting sections and do all the cutting before you begin.

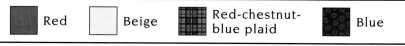

| Red | Beige | Red-chestnut-blue plaid | Blue |

Color Play

To create a brighter color scheme for this color variation on Patches and Plaids, I changed the colors in the Nine Patch Blocks from red and dark beige to lighter shades of rose and beige. And in the lattices, a green plaid takes the place of the darker red-chestnut-blue plaid in the lattices in the quilt on page 105.

Nine Patch Blocks

(Make 64)

Cutting

From the red print fabric:
- ✦ Cut twenty 2½ × 44-inch strips

From the beige print fabric:
- ✦ Cut sixteen 2½ × 44-inch strips

Piecing

1 Sew a 2½ × 44-inch red strip to both sides of a 2½ × 44-inch beige strip, as shown in **Diagram 1,** and press. Make eight of Strip Set I, and cut them into a total of 128 segments, each 2½ inches wide, as shown.

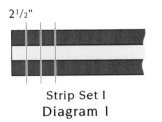

2¹/₂"

Strip Set I
Diagram 1

2 Sew a 2½ × 44-inch beige strip to both sides of a 2½ × 44-inch red strip, as shown in **Diagram 2,** and press. Make four of Strip Set II, and cut them into a total of 64 segments, each 2½ inches wide, as shown.

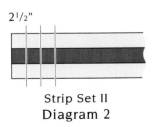

2¹/₂"

Strip Set II
Diagram 2

3 To make the Nine Patch Blocks, sew a Strip Set I seg-

ment to each side of a Strip Set II segment, as shown in **Diagram 3,** and press. Make a total of 64 Nine Patch Blocks. At this point, the Nine Patch Blocks should measure 6½ inches square. Set aside 4 of these blocks to be used in the outer border.

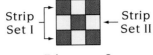

Strip → ← Strip
Set I   Set II

Diagram 3

Triangle-Pieced Square Blocks

(Make 60)

Cutting

From the red-chestnut-blue plaid fabric:
- ✦ Cut six 6⅞ × 44-inch strips

From the beige print fabric:
- ✦ Cut six 6⅞ × 44-inch strips

Piecing

1 Layer the plaid and beige strips together in pairs, and cut the layered strips into thirty 6⅞-inch squares, as shown in **Diagram 4,** taking care not to shift the layers as you cut.

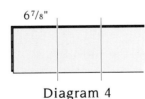

6⁷/₈"

Diagram 4

2 Cut the layered squares in half diagonally, as shown in **Diagram 5.** Stitch ¼ inch away from the diagonal edge, and press. Make a total of 60 Triangle-Pieced Square Blocks.

At this point, the Triangle-Pieced Square Blocks should measure 6½ inches square.

Diagram 5

3 Sew the Nine Patch and Triangle-Pieced Square Blocks together in pairs, as shown in **Diagram 6,** and press.

Diagram 6

4 Sew the pairs of blocks together, as shown in **Diagram 7,** matching the seam intersections. At this point, the blocks should measure 12½ inches square.

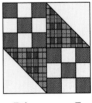

Diagram 7

Quilt Center

Cutting

From the red-chestnut-blue plaid fabric:
- ✦ Cut twenty-four 2½ × 44-inch strips. From these strips, cut seventy-one 2½ × 12½-inch lattice pieces.

From the blue print fabric:
- ✦ Cut three 2½ × 44-inch strips. From these strips, cut forty-two 2½-inch square lattice posts.

Assembly

1 Sew five 2½ × 12½-inch plaid lattice pieces and six 2½-inch square blue lattice posts together for each lattice strip, as shown in **Diagram 8,** and press. Make a total of seven of these lattice strips.

2 Sew five blocks and six 2½ × 12½-inch plaid lattice pieces together for each of the six block rows, as shown in **Diagram 9,** and press.

3 Referring to the **Quilt Diagram,** sew the lattice strips and block rows together, and press.

Diagram 8

Diagram 9

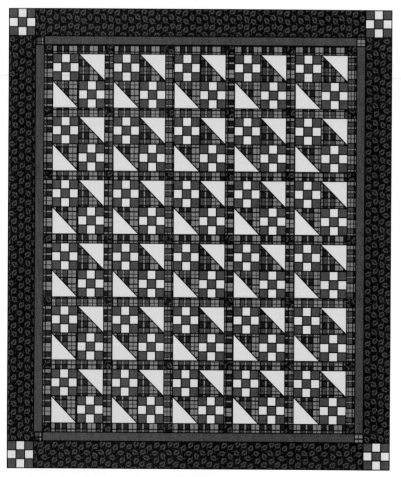

Quilt Diagram

BORDERS

The yardage given allows for the border strips to be cut on the crosswise grain. The border strips are longer than necessary and will be trimmed later.

Cutting

From the red print fabric:
◆ Cut nine 2½ × 44-inch strips for the inner border

From the red-chestnut-blue plaid fabric:
◆ Cut four 2½-inch squares for the corner squares

From the blue print fabric:
◆ Cut nine 6½ × 44-inch strips for the outer border

Attaching the Borders

1 To attach the 2½-inch-wide red top and bottom inner border strips, as shown in the **Quilt Diagram,** refer to page 198 for "Border Instructions."

2 To attach the 2½-inch-wide red side border strips with the 2½-inch square plaid corner squares, as shown in the **Quilt Diagram,** refer to page 200 for "Borders with Corner Squares."

3 To attach the 6½-inch-wide blue top and bottom outer border strips, as shown in the **Quilt Diagram,** refer to page 198 for "Border Instructions."

4 To attach the 6½-inch-wide blue side border strips with Nine Patch corner squares, as shown in the **Quilt Diagram,** refer to page 200 for "Borders with Corner Squares."

PUTTING IT ALL TOGETHER

1 Cut the 8-yard length of backing fabric in thirds crosswise to make three 2⅔-yard lengths. Remove the selvages and sew the long edges together. Press the seam allowances open. Trim the backing and batting so they are about 4 inches larger than the quilt top.

2 For quilting ideas, see the **Quilting Design Diagram.** See page 201 for detailed marking, layering, and finishing instructions.

BINDING

The 2¾-inch binding strips will produce a ½-inch-wide finished binding. If you want a wider or narrower binding, adjust the

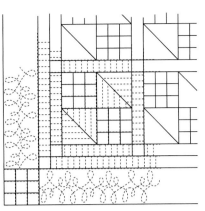

Quilting Design Diagram

width of the strips you cut. (See page 201 for pointers on how to experiment with binding width.) Refer to "Attaching Binding with Mitered Corners" on page 202 to complete your quilt.

Cutting Bias Strips

From the red-chestnut-blue plaid binding fabric:

◆ Cut enough 2¾-inch-wide bias strips to make a 390-inch-long strip

Plan Ahead

Group common sizes of quilting stencils on large, strong binder rings—group large border stencils on one ring, small border stencils on another, and block stencils together on another. Keep your stencils separated by type and size, and hang them on a pegboard wall, or shelf. That way, you'll always have a large supply of quilting designs on hand, and it will be simple to turn the rings and select quilting designs for the Nine Patch Blocks, lattice strips, and borders in Patches and Plaids.

POSTAGE STAMP BASKET

SIZE

Wall Quilt: 68 inches square (unquilted)
Finished Block: 8 inches square

 ## HOUSE DRESSING

See the Checkerboard Bench on top of the larger,
pine-stained bench. Directions are given on page 116.

FABRICS AND SUPPLIES

Yardage is based on 44-inch-wide fabric.

- ✦ 1¼ yards navy print fabric for Basket Blocks, lattice posts, and corner squares

- ✦ 1¼ yards beige print fabric for Basket Blocks background and Checkerboard Strips

- ✦ 1⅓ yards gold print fabric for Checkerboard Strips and inner border

- ✦ 1¾ yards red print fabric for lattice strips

- ✦ 1¼ yards large floral print fabric for outer border

- ✦ ⅔ yard navy print fabric for binding

- ✦ 4 yards fabric for quilt backing

- ✦ Quilt batting, at least 72 inches square

- ✦ Rotary cutter, mat, and wide see-through ruler with ⅛-inch markings

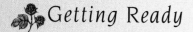
* Read instructions thoroughly before you begin.

* Prewash and press fabric.

* Place right sides of fabric pieces together and use ¼-inch seam allowances throughout unless directions specify otherwise.

* Seam allowances are included in the cutting sizes given.

* Press seam allowances in the direction that will create the least bulk, and whenever possible, press toward the darker fabric. Press border seam allowances toward the borders unless directions specify otherwise.

* Cutting directions for each section of the quilt are given individually. If you like to cut as you go, simply follow the directions as you get to them. If you'd rather cut all your pieces at the same time, skip ahead to find each of the cutting sections and do all the cutting before you begin.

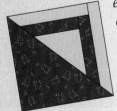

FABRIC KEY
(for the quilt shown on page 111)

| Navy | Beige | Gold | Red | Large floral |

BASKET BLOCKS
(Make 16)

Cutting

From the navy print fabric:

✦ Cut two 8⅞ × 44-inch strips. From these strips, cut eight 8⅞-inch squares. Cut these squares in half diagonally to form 16 triangles.

✦ Cut six 1½ × 44-inch strips

From the beige print fabric:

✦ Cut one 4⅞ × 44-inch strip. From this strip, cut eight 4⅞-inch squares. Cut these squares in half diagonally to form 16 triangles.

✦ Cut eight 1½ × 44-inch strips

Piecing

1 Sew a 1½-inch-wide navy strip to the left side of a beige triangle, as shown in **Diagram 1,** and press. Repeat with the remaining triangles, trimming the navy strips even with the edges of the triangles, as shown.

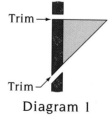

Diagram 1

2 In the same manner, sew a 1½-inch-wide navy strip to the top side of each of the beige triangles, as shown in **Diagram 2,** and press. Trim the navy strips, as shown, to complete the basket handle units.

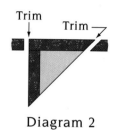

Diagram 2

3 Sew a 1½-inch-wide beige strip to the left side of each of the basket handle units, as shown in **Diagram 3,** and press. Trim the beige strips, as shown.

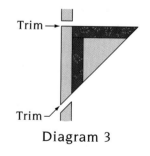

Diagram 3

4 Sew a 1½-inch-wide beige strip to the top of each basket handle unit as shown in **Diagram 4,** press, and trim, as shown.

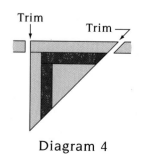

Diagram 4

5 Sew the basket handle units and the navy triangles together, as shown in **Diagram 5,** being careful not to stretch the bias edges as you stitch. Press the seam allowances toward the navy triangles. Make a total of 16 Basket Blocks. At this point, the Basket Blocks should measure 8½ inches square.

Diagram 5

CHECKERBOARD STRIPS

Cutting

From the beige print fabric:

✦ Cut seven 2½ × 44-inch strips

✦ Cut one more 2½ × 44-inch strip. From this strip, cut eight 2½-inch squares.

From the gold print fabric:

✦ Cut seven 2½ × 44-inch strips

✦ Cut one more 2½ × 44-inch strip. From this strip, cut twelve 2½-inch squares.

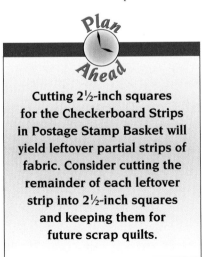

Plan Ahead

Cutting 2½-inch squares for the Checkerboard Strips in Postage Stamp Basket will yield leftover partial strips of fabric. Consider cutting the remainder of each leftover strip into 2½-inch squares and keeping them for future scrap quilts.

Piecing

1 Sew the beige and gold 2½-inch-wide strips together in pairs, as shown in **Diagram 6,** and press, for a total of seven strip sets. Cross cut these strip sets into one hundred and four 2½-inch segments, as shown.

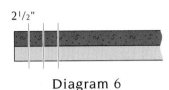

2½"

Diagram 6

2 Referring to **Diagram 7,** sew two Step 1 segments together, and press. Sew a Basket Block to each side of this unit, as shown, and press. Refer to the diagram for proper placement of the basket handles and the checkerboard segments. Make a total of eight of these basket units.

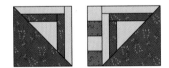

Diagram 7

3 Sew four Step 1 segments together, as shown at the top of **Diagram 8.** Sew a 2½-inch gold square to the end of this unit, as shown, and press. Repeat to make four of these Checkerboard Strips.

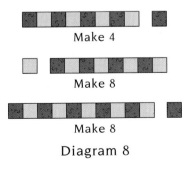

Make 4

Make 8

Make 8

Diagram 8

4 Referring to the middle of **Diagram 8,** sew four Step 1 segments together. Add a 2½-inch beige square to the end of this unit, as shown, and press. Repeat to make eight of these Checkerboard Strips.

5 Referring to the bottom of **Diagram 8,** sew five Step 1 segments together. Add a 2½-inch gold square to the end of this unit, as shown, and press. Repeat to make eight of these Checkerboard Strips.

6 Referring to **Diagram 9,** sew a Step 2 basket unit to each side of the Checkerboard Strip shown at the top of **Diagram 8,** and press. Repeat to make four of these basket sections, as shown.

Diagram 9

7 Referring to **Diagram 9,** sew a Checkerboard Strip from the middle of **Diagram 8** to the top and bottom of each of the four basket sections, and press.

8 Referring to **Diagram 9,** sew a Checkerboard Strip from the bottom of **Diagram 8** to the sides of each of the four basket sections, and press. At this point, each of the four basket and checkerboard units should measure 22½ inches square.

Quilt Center

Cutting

From the red print fabric:
- Cut twelve 4½ × 22½-inch lattice strips

From the navy print fabric:
- Cut nine 4½-inch square lattice posts

Assembly

1 Sew three 4½ × 22½-inch red lattice strips and two basket/checkerboard sections together in a row, as shown at the top of **Diagram 10,** and press. Make two of these rows.

2 Referring to the bottom of **Diagram 10,** sew two 4½ × 22½-inch red lattice strips and three 4½-inch square navy lattice posts together, and press. Make three of these strips.

3 Stitch the rows and strips together to form the quilt center, as shown in **Diagram 11.**

Borders

The yardage given allows for the border strips to be cut on the crosswise grain. The border strips are longer than necessary and will be trimmed later.

Cutting

From the gold print fabric:
- Cut six 2½ × 44-inch strips for the inner border

From the navy print fabric:
- Cut four 2½-inch corner squares

From the large floral print fabric:
- Cut eight 4½ × 44-inch strips for the outer border

Attaching the Borders

1 To attach the 2½-inch-wide gold top and bottom inner border strips, as shown in the **Quilt Diagram** on page 115, refer to page 198 for "Border Instructions."

2 To attach the 2½-inch-wide gold side borders with navy corner squares, as shown in the **Quilt Diagram,** refer to page 200 for "Borders with Corner Squares."

3 To attach the 4½-inch-wide large floral outer border strips, as shown in the **Quilt Diagram,** refer to page 198 for "Border Instructions."

Diagram 10

Diagram 11

Quilt Diagram

PUTTING IT ALL TOGETHER

1 Cut the 4-yard length of backing fabric in half crosswise to make two 2-yard lengths. Remove the selvages, and sew the long edges together. Press the seam allowances open. Trim the backing and batting so they are about 4 inches larger than the quilt top.

2 For quilting ideas, see the **Quilting Design Diagram.** See page 201 for detailed marking, layering, and finishing instructions.

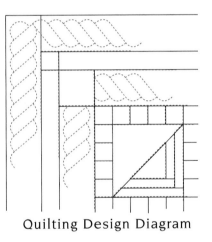

Quilting Design Diagram

BINDING

The 2¾-inch binding strips will produce a ½-inch-wide finished binding. If you want a wider or narrower binding, adjust the width of the strips you cut. (See page 201 for pointers on how to experiment with binding width.) Refer to "Attaching Binding with Mitered Corners" on page 202 to complete your quilt.

Cutting Crosswise Strips

From the navy print binding fabric:

✦ Cut seven 2¾ × 44-inch strips on the crosswise grain

SUPPLIES

All supplies are available from hobby or craft stores.

+ Wooden bench

+ Latex paint

+ Template plastic

+ Stencil paints for walls

+ Wooden skewer

+ Medium sandpaper (optional)

+ Walnut wood stain

+ Matte polyurethane or varnish and brush

1 Paint the bench with latex paint, and allow it to dry for 4 hours.

2 Cut a checkerboard stencil out of template plastic, by spacing a row of several 1½-inch squares 1½ inches apart (or use a purchased checkerboard stencil, if desired).

3 Using stencil paint for walls, paint two rows of squares on the bottom front side of the bench, staggering the squares to create a checkerboard pattern. Paint checkerboard squares over the entire surface of the bench top.

4 With a contrasting color, paint the edges of the bench top. Dip the blunt end of the wooden skewer into the same color paint, and lightly dab a dot of color at the corners of the stenciled squares on both the bottom front and the top of the bench.

5 With medium sandpaper, lightly sand all of the edges of the bench and the bench top to expose the raw wood, if desired.

6 With walnut wood stain and a clean rag, rub stain over the entire bench. Wipe off the excess stain, and allow it to dry for 24 hours.

7 To seal the surface of the bench, paint it with matte polyurethane or varnish.

Susie Lenz
Quilt Teacher

My Life When I'm Not Quilting

Working and teaching classes in a quilt shop give me a chance to see a wide array of quilts and become familiar with lots of new quiltmaking techniques. Although I personally love making traditional-style quilts, I enjoy seeing projects that range all the way from contemporary art quilts to more casual, country-style designs. I also make samples and check patterns for quilt pattern companies, including Pine Tree Lodge Designs, Simple Pleasures Patterns, and Brandywine Designs, checking measurements to make sure that things will fit together correctly. In addition to the enjoyment I get from this kind of work, it also helps expand my repertoire of quilt-making skills.

Why I Quilt

When I'm working or teaching in the quilt shop, I'm involved in helping other people with their projects, so I really enjoy doing things for myself at home. Quilting fosters my ability to be creative, and it gives me a lot of confidence to see something I make turn out well.

My Most Memorable Project

Birds and Blooms from *The Thimbleberries Book of Quilts* was my first attempt at appliqué. Because the shapes were large and easy to stitch, without any sharp points, it was a very successful first project—and that is what gave me the encouragement to continue making more quilts.

Adding your own original appliqué designs or using a completely different color combination can make a quilt really come alive.

—Susie Lenz

STAR-SPANGLED TREE SKIRT

SIZE

Tree Skirt: 54 inches square (unquilted)

 ## HOUSE DRESSING

See the Holiday Gift Bags on the table.
Directions are given on page 124.

FABRICS AND SUPPLIES

Yardage is based on 44-inch-wide fabric.

+ 1¼ yards gold plaid fabric for stars

+ ¾ yard beige print fabric for Center Star Block background

+ 1 yard green print fabric for Corner Star Blocks and pieced border

+ 1½ yards red print fabric for Corner Star Blocks, pieced border, and outer border

+ ⅔ yard brown print fabric for pieced border

+ ¾ yard green print fabric for binding and ties

+ 3¼ yards fabric for tree skirt backing

+ Quilt batting, at least 58 inches square

+ Rotary cutter, mat, and wide see-through ruler with ⅛-inch markings

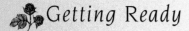
✿ Read instructions thoroughly before you begin.

✿ Prewash and press fabric.

✿ Place right sides of fabric pieces together and use ¼-inch seam allowances throughout unless directions specify otherwise.

✿ Seam allowances are included in the cutting sizes given.

✿ Press seam allowances in the direction that will create the least bulk, and whenever possible, press toward the darker fabric. Press border seam allowances toward the borders unless directions specify otherwise.

✿ Cutting directions for each section of the quilt are given individually. If you like to cut as you go, simply follow the directions as you get to them. If you'd rather cut all your pieces at the same time, skip ahead to find each of the cutting sections and do all the cutting before you begin.

FABRIC KEY
(for the quilt shown on page 119)

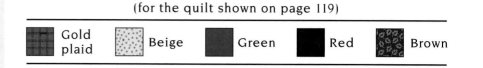

| Gold plaid | Beige | Green | Red | Brown |

CENTER STAR BLOCK
(Make 1)

Cutting

From the gold plaid fabric:
◆ Cut one 12½-inch square

◆ Cut eight 6½-inch squares

From the beige print fabric:
◆ Cut four 6½ × 12½-inch rectangles

◆ Cut four 6½-inch squares

Plan Ahead

When purchasing the fabrics for Star-Spangled Tree Skirt, consider buying enough to make *two* tree skirts. That way you can cut all of the pieces for both tree skirts at the same time, and set the extras aside to make either a coordinating table covering (omit cutting the center circle) or a great Christmas gift for someone special.

Piecing

1 Position a 6½-inch gold square on the corner of a 6½ × 12½-inch beige rec-

tangle, as shown at top left in **Diagram 1.** Draw a diagonal line on the gold square, and stitch on the line. Trim away the excess corner fabric, leaving a ¼-inch seam allowance, and press, as shown at top right. Repeat at the opposite corner of the beige rectangle, creating a star point unit, as shown at lower right in the diagram. Repeat for each of the remaining 6½ × 12½-inch beige rectangles.

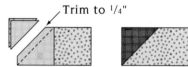

Trim to ¹/₄"

Trim to ¹/₄"

Diagram 1

2 Sew a star point unit to the top and one to the bottom of the 12½-inch gold square, as shown in **Diagram 2,** and press.

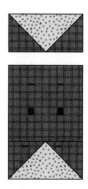

Diagram 2

3 Sew a 6½-inch beige square to each end of the two remaining star point units, as shown in **Diagram 3,** and press.

Diagram 3

4 Sew one of the Step 3 units to each side of the Step 2 unit, as shown in **Diagram 4.** At this point, the Center Star Block should measure 24½ inches square.

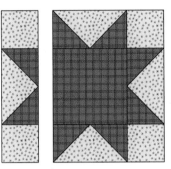

Diagram 4

CORNER STAR BLOCKS

(Make 4)

Cutting

From the gold plaid fabric:

+ Cut four 6½-inch squares

+ Cut three 3½ × 44-inch strips. From these strips, cut thirty-two 3½-inch squares.

From the green print fabric:

+ Cut three 3½ × 44-inch strips. From these strips, cut eight 3½ × 6½-inch rectangles and sixteen 3½-inch squares.

From the red print fabric:

+ Cut two 3½ × 44-inch strips. From these strips, cut eight 3½ × 6½-inch rectangles.

Piecing

1 Position a 3½-inch gold square on the corner of a 3½ × 6½-inch green rectangle, as shown at top left in **Diagram 5.** Draw a diagonal line on the gold square, and stitch on the line. Trim away excess corner fabric, leaving a ¼-inch seam allowance, and press, as shown at top right. Repeat at the opposite corner to create a star point unit, as shown at lower right in the diagram. Repeat to make a total of eight green and gold star point units.

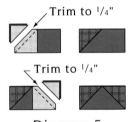

Diagram 5

2 Using 3½-inch gold squares and 3½ × 6½-inch red rectangles, repeat Step 1 to make a total of eight red and gold star point units, as shown at lower right in **Diagram 6.**

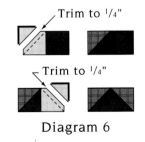

Diagram 6

3 Sew a Step 1 star point unit to one side of each of the 6½-inch gold squares, as shown in **Diagram 7,** and press. Sew a Step 2 star point unit to the opposite side of each of the gold squares, as shown, and press.

Diagram 7

4 Sew a 3½-inch green square to both ends of the remaining Step 1 and Step 2 star point units, as shown in **Diagram 8,** and press.

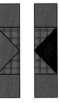

Diagram 8

5 Sew a green star point unit from Step 4 to one side of the Corner Star Block, as shown in **Diagram 9.** Sew a red star point unit from Step 4 to the opposite side of the block, as shown, and press. Make a total of four Corner Star Blocks. At this point, the Corner Star Blocks should measure 12½ inches square.

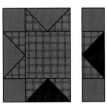

Diagram 9

BORDERS

The yardage given allows for the border strips to be cut on the crosswise grain. The border strips are longer than necessary and will be trimmed later.

Cutting

From the green print fabric:
✦ Cut five 3½ × 44-inch strips for the pieced border

From the red print fabric:
✦ Cut two 7¼ × 44-inch strips. From these strips, cut eight 7¼-inch squares. Cut the squares diagonally into quarters, forming thirty-two triangles for the pieced border.

✦ Cut six 3½ × 44-inch strips for the outer border

From the brown print fabric:
✦ Cut two 7¼ × 44-inch strips. From these strips, cut eight 7¼-inch squares. Cut the squares diagonally into quarters, forming thirty-two triangles for the pieced border.

Piecing

1 Layer a red triangle on a brown triangle, as shown at left in **Diagram 10.** Sew a ¼-inch seam along the bias edge, as shown, being careful not to stretch the fabric as you stitch. Repeat for each of the remaining brown and red triangles, making sure to sew along the same bias edge of each triangle set, so that the pieced triangle units will all have the red triangles on the same side, and press.

Diagram 10

2 Sew the Step 1 pieced triangle units together in pairs, as shown at right in **Diagram 10,** and press. At this point, the triangle blocks should measure 6½ inches square.

3 Sew four triangle blocks together, as shown at the middle of **Diagram 11,** and press. At this point, the pieced triangle strips should measure 6½ × 24½ inches.

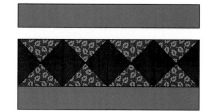

Diagram 11

4 Sew the 3½ × 44-inch green strips together with diagonal seams. For more information on diagonal seams, see page 198. Trim the seam allowances to ¼ inch, and press them open. Cut eight 3½ × 24½-inch strips. Sew a green strip to both sides of each pieced triangle strip, as shown in **Diagram 11,** and press.

5 Sew a pieced border strip to the top and bottom of the Center Star Block, referring to the **Tree Skirt Diagram,** and press.

6 Referring to the **Tree Skirt Diagram,** sew a Corner Star Block to each end of the two remaining pieced border strips, and press. Sew these pieced border strips to the sides of the quilt, as shown, and press.

Attaching the Outer Border

To attach the 3½-inch-wide red outer border strips, as shown in the **Tree Skirt Diagram,** refer to page 198 for "Border Instructions."

Tree Skirt Diagram

PUTTING IT ALL TOGETHER

1 Cut the 3¼-yard length of backing fabric in half crosswise to make two 1⅝-yard lengths. Remove the selvages, and sew the long edges together. Press the seam allowances open. Trim the backing and batting so they are about 4 inches larger than the quilt top.

2 For quilting ideas, see the **Quilting Design Diagram.** When the quilting is complete, remove the basting stitches, and trim the excess backing and batting even with the edges of the tree skirt top.

3 Use the Center Circle Template A on page 125 to draw a 4¾-inch-diameter circle at the center of the tree skirt, referring to the **Tree Skirt Diagram** on page 122. Draw a straight line from the circle to the midpoint of one edge of the tree skirt, as shown.

4 Referring to the **Tree Skirt Diagram,** machine stitch ¼ inch outside the circle and ¼ inch on either side of the straight line. Cut on the straight line and around the circle, as shown.

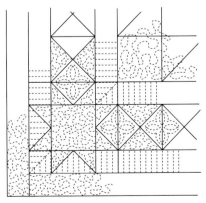

Quilting Design Diagram

BINDING

The 2¾-inch binding strips will produce a ½-inch-wide finished binding. If you want a wider or narrower binding, adjust the width of the strips you cut. (See page 201 for pointers on how to experiment with binding width.)

Cutting Crosswise Strips

From the green print binding fabric:
◆ Cut seven 2¾ × 44-inch strips on the crosswise grain for the outer edges of the tree skirt

Cutting Bias Strips

From the green print binding fabric:
◆ Cut enough 2½-inch-wide bias strips to make a 56-inch-long strip for the center circle and ties

Attaching the Binding

1 Sew the binding strips for the outer edges of the tree skirt together with diagonal seams. Trim the seam allowances to ¼ inch, and press them open.

2 Fold the binding strip in half lengthwise, wrong sides together, and press.

3 Referring to **Diagram 12,** sew the binding to the tree skirt with a ⅜-inch-wide seam, beginning and ending at the center circle, and mitering the corners. For detailed information on mitering corners, see "Attaching Binding with Mitered Corners" on page 202.

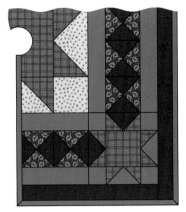

Diagram 12

4 Turn the binding to the back side of the tree skirt and hand stitch it in place.

5 Bind the center opening of the tree skirt in the same way, using the bias binding strips and a ¼-inch seam allowance.

NOTE: *A narrower seam allowance will make this binding easier to handle.*

Allow 20 inches of binding to extend beyond each opening edge to serve as ties, as shown in **Diagram 13.** Hand stitch the folded edges of the binding together along the tie extensions, turning in the raw ends as you go.

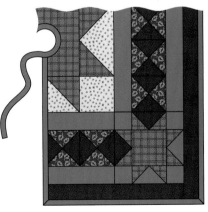

Diagram 13

HOUSE DRESSING

Holiday Gift Bag

FABRICS AND SUPPLIES

- 11 × 28-inch fabric for bag
- Appliqué shapes from My Favorite Things, pages 35–39
- Paper-backed fusible web
- Scraps of colorful fabrics for appliqués
- Black pearl cotton/fine-tip permanent marker (optional)

1 Pull out several threads along both of the short ends of the 11 × 28-inch piece of bag fabric to create a ½-inch fringed edge.

2 With right sides together, fold the bag fabric in half crosswise, as shown in **Diagram 1,** sew the side seams, and press these seams open.

Diagram 1

3 To create a flat bottom, turn the bag so that the right sides are facing each other. Match the side seams to the fold line on the bottom of the bag, as shown in **Diagram 2.** Sew across both triangles, approximately 2 inches down from the point, as shown. Turn the bag right side out.

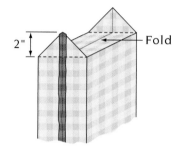

Diagram 2

4 Trace the appliqué shapes you like from pages 35–39 onto the paper side of the fusible web. Cut roughly around the appliqué shapes. Following the manufacturer's directions, apply the fusible web to the wrong sides of your appliqué fabrics. Cut out each appliqué shape on your traced lines, and peel off the paper backing.

5 Fuse the appliqué shapes on the front of the bag. Appliqué them in place by hand or machine, or use a Pigma black permanent fabric marker to penstitch them and eliminate the stitching entirely.

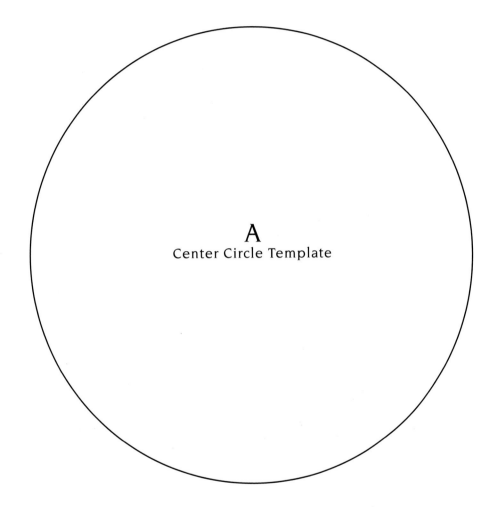

A
Center Circle Template

HUGS AND KISSES

SIZE

Crib Quilt: 46 × 58 inches (unquilted)
Finished Blocks: 10 inches square

FABRICS AND SUPPLIES

Yardage is based on 44-inch-wide fabric.

+ ¾ yard blue print fabric for Hugs Blocks

+ ⅔ yard red print fabric for Kisses Blocks

+ ½ yard gold print fabric for center squares, lattice posts, and corner squares

+ 1 yard beige print fabric for background

+ ⅞ yard red plaid fabric for lattice pieces

+ ⅞ yard brown print fabric for border

+ ¾ yard blue print fabric for binding

+ 2¾ yards fabric for quilt backing

+ Quilt batting, at least 50 × 62 inches

+ Rotary cutter, mat, and wide see-through ruler with ⅛-inch markings

Color Play

See page 128 for a creative color variation
on the quilt shown here.

Getting Ready

❧ Read instructions thoroughly before you begin.

❧ Prewash and press fabric.

❧ Place right sides of fabric pieces together and use ¼-inch seam allowances throughout unless directions specify otherwise.

❧ Seam allowances are included in the cutting sizes given.

❧ Press seam allowances in the direction that will create the least bulk, and whenever possible, press toward the darker fabric. Press border seam allowances toward the borders unless directions specify otherwise.

❧ Cutting directions for each section of the quilt are given individually. If you like to cut as you go, simply follow the directions as you get to them. If you'd rather cut all your pieces at the same time, skip ahead to find each of the cutting sections and do all the cutting before you begin.

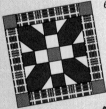

FABRIC KEY
(for the quilt shown on page 127)

⬛ Blue		🟥 Red print	
🟫 Gold	⬜ Beige	Red plaid	⬛ Brown

Color Play

Changing the bright red in the Kisses Blocks to a mellow green and substituting a small red check for the bold blue in the Hugs Blocks help to create a softer color palette for this color variation quilt. A playful children's print with a yellow background makes this a perfect choice for a child's room.

HUGS BLOCKS

(Make 6)

Cutting

From the blue print fabric:

+ Cut two 2½ × 17-inch strips

+ Cut three 2½ × 44-inch strips. From these strips, cut twelve 2½ × 10½-inch rectangles.

+ Cut three more 2½ × 44-inch strips. From these strips, cut twenty-four 2½ × 4½-inch rectangles.

From the gold print fabric:

+ Cut one 2½ × 17-inch strip

From the beige print fabric:

+ Cut two 2½ × 17-inch strips

+ Cut four 2½ × 44-inch strips. From these strips, cut sixty 2½-inch squares.

Piecing

1 Sew two 2½ × 17-inch blue strips, two 2½ × 17-inch beige strips, and one 2½ × 17-inch gold strip together, as shown in **Diagram 1,** and press. Cross cut the strip set into six 2½-inch segments, as shown.

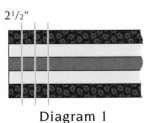

2½"

Diagram 1

2 Position a 2½-inch beige square on the corners of each of the 2½ × 10½-inch blue rectangles, as shown at the top of **Diagram 2.** Stitch diagonally from corner to corner on the beige squares, as shown. Trim the seam allowances to ¼ inch, and press, as shown at the bottom of the diagram. Repeat to make 12 of these units.

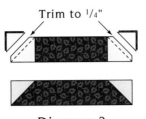

Trim to ¼"

Diagram 2

3 Position a 2½-inch beige square on the 2½ × 4½-inch blue rectangles, as shown at top left in **Diagram 3.** Stitch diagonally from corner to corner on the beige squares, as shown. Trim the seam allowances to ¼ inch, and press. Make 12 of these units with points positioned as shown at top right in the diagram. Reverse the direction of the diagonal line when sewing the remaining 12 units, to position the points as shown at lower right in the diagram.

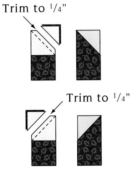

Trim to ¼"

Trim to ¼"

Diagram 3

4 Sew a 2½-inch beige square between a left-point unit and a right-point unit, as shown in **Diagram 4,** and press. Make a total of 12 of these units.

Diagram 4

Plan Ahead

If you like to cut all of the pieces for a quilt at the same time, stack your cut pieces so that they correspond to the way the pattern is written—that is, the order in which you will be using them. Use a permanent marker to mark pieces of masking tape, and label each stack according to where it will be placed in the quilt—for example, the Hugs or Kisses Blocks, lattice posts, lattice pieces, or border corner squares.

5 Referring to **Diagram 5,** stitch the segments from Steps 1, 2, and 4 together, and press. Make a total of six Hugs Blocks. At this point, each block should measure 10½ inches square.

Hugs Block
Diagram 5

KISSES BLOCKS

(Make 6)

Cutting

From the red print fabric:

+ Cut two 2½ × 17-inch strips

+ Cut one 2½ × 44-inch strip

+ Cut three 4½ × 44-inch strips. From these strips, cut twenty-four 4½-inch squares.

From the gold print fabric:
✦ Cut one 2½ × 17-inch strip

From the beige print fabric:
✦ Cut two 2½ × 17-inch strips

✦ Cut one 2½ × 44-inch strip

✦ Cut three more 2½ × 44-inch strips. From these strips, cut forty-eight 2½-inch squares.

Piecing

1 Sew two 2½ × 17-inch red strips, two 2½ × 17-inch beige strips, and one 2½ × 17-inch gold strip together, as shown in **Diagram 6,** and press. Cross cut the strip set into six 2½-inch segments, as shown.

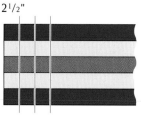

2½"

Diagram 6

2 Sew the 2½ × 44-inch red and beige strips together, as shown in **Diagram 7,** and press. Cross cut this strip set into twelve 2½-inch segments, as shown.

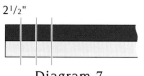

2½"

Diagram 7

3 Position a 2½-inch beige square on opposite corners of each of the 4½-inch red squares, as shown in **Diagram 8.** Stitch diagonally from corner to corner on the beige squares,

as shown. Trim the seam allowances to ¼ inch, and press. Make a total of 24 of these units.

Trim to ¼"

Diagram 8

4 Referring to **Diagram 9,** stitch the segments from Steps 1, 2, and 3 together, and press. Make a total of six Kisses Blocks. At this point, each block should measure 10½ inches square.

Kisses Block
Diagram 9

QUILT CENTER

Cutting

From the red plaid fabric:
✦ Cut eight 2½ × 44-inch strips. From these strips, cut thirty-one 2½ × 10½-inch lattice pieces.

From the gold print fabric:
✦ Cut two 2½ × 44-inch strips. From these strips, cut twenty 2½-inch square lattice posts.

Piecing

1 Sew three 2½ × 10½-inch red plaid lattice pieces and four 2½-inch square gold lattice posts together, as shown in **Diagram 10,** and press. Make five of these lattice strips.

2 Referring to the **Quilt Diagram** on page 131 for block placement, sew the Hugs and Kisses Blocks, and four red plaid lattice pieces together to form four horizontal rows. Two of the four rows start and end with Hugs Blocks and two rows start and end with Kisses Blocks.

3 Referring to the **Quilt Diagram,** sew the four horizontal rows and five lattice strips together, and press.

BORDERS

The yardage given allows for the border strips to be cut on the crosswise grain. The border strips are longer than necessary and will be trimmed later.

Cutting

From the brown print fabric:
✦ Cut five 4½ × 44-inch strips for the border

From the gold print fabric:
✦ Cut four 4½-inch corner squares

Attaching the Border

1 To attach the 4½-inch-wide brown top and bottom border

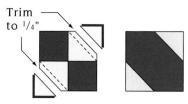

Diagram 10

Quilt Diagram

strips, as shown in the **Quilt Diagram,** refer to page 198 for "Border Instructions."

2 To attach the 4½-inch-wide brown side border strips with gold corner squares, as shown in the **Quilt Diagram,** refer to page 200 for "Borders with Corner Squares."

PUTTING IT ALL TOGETHER

1 Cut the 2¾-yard length of backing fabric in half crosswise to make two 1⅜-yard lengths. Remove the selvages and sew the long edges together. Press the seam allowances open. Trim the backing and batting so they are about 4 inches larger than the quilt top.

2 For quilting ideas, see the **Quilting Design Diagram.** See page 201 for detailed marking, layering, and finishing instructions.

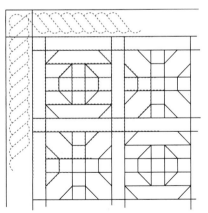

Quilting Design Diagram

Binding

The 2¾-inch binding strips will produce a ½-inch-wide finished binding. If you want a wider or narrower binding, adjust the width of the strips you cut. (See page 201 for pointers on how to experiment with binding width.) Refer to "Attaching Binding with Mitered Corners" on page 202 to complete your quilt.

Cutting Crosswise Strips

From the blue print binding fabric:

✦ Cut six 2¾ × 44-inch strips on the crosswise grain

FLURRIES

SIZE

Wall Quilt: 48 × 64 inches (unquilted)
Finished Block: 14 × 22 inches

 ## HOUSE DRESSING

See the Soft-Sculpture Bag on the bench near the wall quilt.
Directions are given on page 139.

FABRICS AND SUPPLIES

Yardage is based on 44-inch-wide fabric.

+ 1 yard beige print fabric for background

+ ⅝ yard brown print fabric for checkerboard

+ ¾ yard black print fabric for checkerboard and lattice posts

+ ¼ yard green print #1 fabric for tall tree appliqués

+ ¼ yard green print #2 fabric for shorter tree appliqués

+ ¼ yard cream print fabric for snowflake appliqués

+ 1½ yards red print fabric for lattice pieces and outer border

+ 2 yards paper-backed fusible web

+ One spool #8 DMC black pearl cotton

+ ⅝ yard green print #2 fabric for binding

+ 3 yards fabric for quilt backing

+ Quilt batting, at least 52 × 68 inches

+ Rotary cutter, mat, and wide see-through ruler with ⅛-inch markings

Getting Ready

❋ Read instructions thoroughly before you begin.

❋ Note that the appliqué in this project is done using the fusible appliqué method.

❋ Prewash and press fabric.

❋ Place right sides of fabric pieces together and use ¼-inch seam allowances throughout unless directions specify otherwise.

❋ Seam allowances are included in the cutting sizes given.

❋ Press seam allowances in the direction that will create the least bulk, and whenever possible, press toward the darker fabric. Press border seam allowances toward the borders unless directions specify otherwise.

❋ Cutting directions for each section of the quilt are given individually. If you like to cut as you go, simply follow the directions as you get to them. If you'd rather cut all your pieces at the same time, skip ahead to find each of the cutting sections and do all the cutting before you begin.

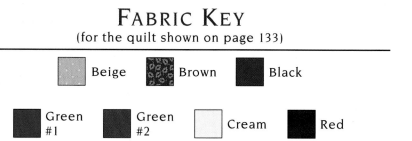

Beige   Brown   Black

Green #1   Green #2   Cream   Red

CHECKERBOARD SECTION

Cutting

From the brown print fabric:
✦ Cut six 2½ × 44-inch strips

From the black print fabric:
✦ Cut six 2½ × 44-inch strips

Piecing

1 Sew a 2½ × 44-inch black strip to each side of two 2½ × 44-inch brown strips, as shown in **Diagram 1.** Make two of Strip Set I, and cross cut them into thirty-two 2½-inch segments, as shown.

2½"

Strip Set I

Diagram 1

2 Sew a 2½ × 44-inch brown strip to each side of two 2½ × 44-inch black strips, as shown in **Diagram 2.** Make two of Strip Set II, and cross cut them into twenty-six 2½-inch segments, as shown.

2½"

Strip Set II

Diagram 2

3 Sew four Strip Set I segments and three Strip Set II segments together, as shown in **Diagram 3,** and press. Make a total of four of these checkerboard units.

Diagram 3

4 Set the remaining Strip Set I and II segments aside, to be used later in the checkerboard border.

APPLIQUÉD BLOCKS
(Make 4)

Cutting

From the beige print fabric:
✦ Cut four 14½ × 16½-inch rectangles

Appliquéing

1 Position the fusible web (paper side facing up) over the appliqué shapes on pages 137–138. Trace 4 A Trees, 8 B Trees, and 12 C Snowflakes onto the fusible web, leaving at least ½ inch between each shape.

2 Roughly cut around the traced shapes, as shown in **Diagram 4.**

It's easier to appliqué on blocks than on assembled quilts, but when shapes overlap seams, this isn't always possible. For Flurries, do the appliqué on the center part of the quilt before you attach the borders.

NOTE: *When you are fusing a large shape, like the large A Tree, fuse just the outer edges of the shape, so that it will not look stiff when finished. To do this, draw a line about ⅜ inch inside the tree, and cut away the fusible web on this line, as shown.*

Cut away

Diagram 4

3 Following the manufacturer's instructions, fuse the shapes to the wrong side of the fabrics, as shown in **Diagram 5.** Let the fabric cool, and cut along the outline of each shape, as shown. Peel away the paper from the fusible web.

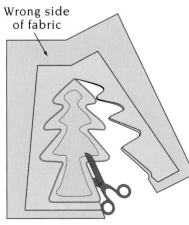

Wrong side of fabric

Diagram 5

4 Sew the 14½ × 16½-inch beige rectangles to the checkerboard units, and press the seam allowances away from the checkerboard.

5 Position the A and B Trees on the beige rectangles ¼ inch above the checkerboards, as shown in **Diagram 6,** making sure that the B Trees are at least ½ inch from the edge of the rectangles. Wait to position the C Snowflake appliqués until *after* you have assembled the quilt center, because they will overlap the lattice seam lines.

Diagram 6

6 Using the buttonhole stitch and one strand of pearl cotton, appliqué the shapes in place. Refer to page 197 for "Decorative Stitches."

QUILT CENTER

Cutting

From the red print fabric:

◆ Cut six 2½ × 44-inch strips. From these strips, cut six 2½ × 22½-inch rectangles for lattice pieces and six 2½ × 14½-inch rectangles for lattice pieces.

From the black print fabric:

◆ Cut nine 2½-inch squares for lattice posts

Assembly

1 Sew two 2½ × 14½-inch red lattice pieces and three 2½-inch square black lattice posts together, as shown in **Diagram 7.** Make three of these lattice strips, and press.

2 Sew two appliquéd blocks and three 2½ × 22½-inch red lattice pieces together, as shown in **Diagram 8,** and press. Repeat, using the remaining appliquéd blocks and lattice pieces.

Diagram 7

Diagram 8

3 Referring to the **Quilt Diagram,** sew the block rows and lattice strips together. Press the seam allowances toward the lattice strips.

4 Referring to the **Quilt Diagram,** position the middle snowflake in each block so that it extends 1 inch into the lattice piece above the block, as shown. Position the side snowflakes in each block so they are 2¼ inches from the top of the beige background rectangles, and they extend ½ inch into the side lattice pieces, as shown. When everything is in position, fuse the snowflake appliqués in place.

5 Using the buttonhole stitch and one strand of pearl cotton, appliqué the snowflakes in place on the quilt center. Refer to page 197 for "Decorative Stitches."

BORDERS

The yardage given allows for the border strips to be cut on the crosswise grain. The border strips are longer than necessary and will be trimmed later.

Cutting

From the red print fabric:
✦ Cut six 5½ × 44-inch strips for the outer border

Piecing

1 Sew three Strip Set I segments and three Strip Set II segments together, as shown in **Diagram 9.** Remove the final black square from the checkerboard border, as shown. Make a total of two of these borders, sew them to the top and bottom of the quilt, and press.

2 Sew five Strip Set I segments and four Strip Set II segments together, as shown in **Diagram 10,** and press. Make a total of two of these borders, sew them to the sides of the quilt, and press.

3 To attach the 5½-inch-wide red outer border strips, as shown in the **Quilt Diagram,** refer to page 198 for "Border Instructions."

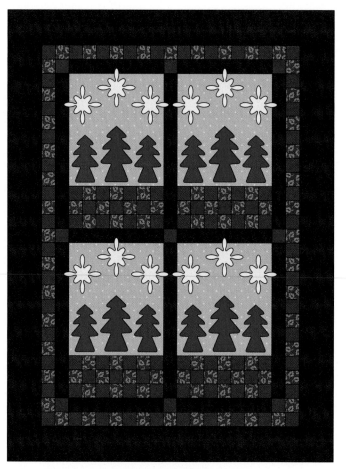

Quilt Diagram

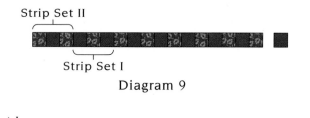

Strip Set II

Strip Set I

Diagram 9

Strip Set I

Strip Set II

Diagram 10

PUTTING IT ALL TOGETHER

1 Cut the 3-yard length of backing fabric in half crosswise to make two 1½-yard lengths. Remove the selvages and sew the long edges together. Press the seam allowances open. Trim the backing and batting so they are about 4 inches larger than the quilt top.

2 For quilting ideas, see the **Quilting Design Diagram.** See page 201 for detailed marking, layering, and finishing instructions.

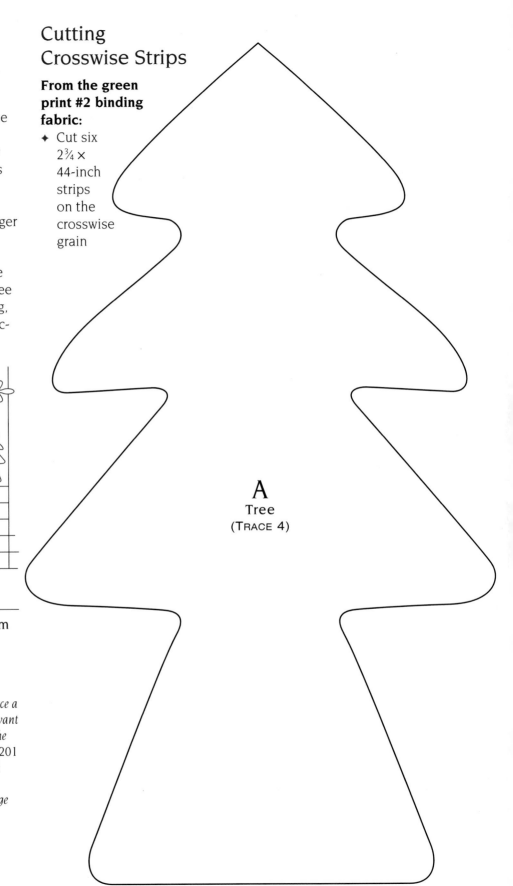

Quilting Design Diagram

BINDING

The 2¾-inch binding strips will produce a ½-inch-wide finished binding. If you want a wider or narrower binding, adjust the width of the strips you cut. (See page 201 for pointers on how to experiment with binding width.) Refer to "Attaching Binding with Mitered Corners" on page 202 to complete your quilt.

Cutting Crosswise Strips

From the green print #2 binding fabric:

◆ Cut six 2¾ × 44-inch strips on the crosswise grain

A
Tree
(TRACE 4)

C
Snowflake
(TRACE 12)

B
Tree
(TRACE 8)

FLURRIES

FABRICS AND SUPPLIES

- Forty-eight 4½-inch squares of assorted fabrics for bag
- Paper-backed fusible web
- ¼ yard beige print fabric for snowflakes
- One spool #8 DMC black pearl cotton
- 36-inch square of quilt batting
- ½ yard green print lining fabric
- ½ yard red plaid fabric for binding, casing, and tie

1 Sew together six of the 4½-inch squares in a random pattern, and press. Make eight of these strips. Sew four strips together for the front and four for the back of the bag.

2 Trace six snowflake shapes from page 138 onto the fusible web. Referring to the fusible web appliqué instructions on page 134, prepare six beige snowflakes. Fuse three snowflakes on the front and three on the back of the bag. Position the lowest snowflake 4¼ inches up from the bottom edge and 3½ inches in from the left side of the bag. Place the middle snowflake 8½ inches up from the bottom and 2½ inches in from the right side of the bag. Place the top snowflake 11 inches up from the bottom and 4 inches in from the left side of the bag. Buttonhole stitch the edges of each snowflake.

3 Cut the batting and the lining fabric into two 18 × 26-inch pieces. Layer the lining, batting, and pieced bag front. Baste the layers together and quilt as desired. Trim the batting and lining even with the bag front. Repeat for the bag back.

4 With right sides together, layer the front and back units. Stitch the sides and bottom together with a ¼-inch seam allowance.

5 With right sides together, match the side seams and the bottom seam, as shown in **Diagram 1.** Stitch across the triangle approximately 2 inches down from each point, as shown. Turn the bag right side out.

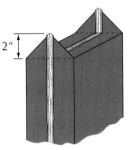

Diagram 1

6 Cut the red plaid fabric into one 3½ × 30-inch bias strip for the binding, one 2 × 28-inch bias strip for a casing, and one 1¾ × 50-inch bias strip for a tie.

7 Press the 3½ × 30-inch bias strip in half lengthwise, wrong sides together. With right sides together and raw edges aligned, sew the bias binding strip to the top of the bag with a ½-inch seam allowance. Fold the binding to the inside of the bag and hand stitch over the seam line.

8 Press under ½ inch along the long edges of the 2 × 28-inch bias strip and baste to the outside of the bag 5½ inches down from the bag top, beginning and ending at a side seam. Turn under the short ends at the side seams, and machine stitch the long edges through all thicknesses, creating a casing.

9 Fold the 1¾ × 50-inch bias strip in half lengthwise, right sides together. Stitch as shown in **Diagram 2,** tapering the ends and leaving an opening in the middle to turn. Trim, turn right side out, and press. Hand stitch the opening closed, and thread the tie through the casing.

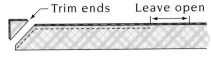

Diagram 2

THIMBLEBERRIES MIX

SIZE

Bed Quilt: 72 × 96 inches (unquilted)
Finished Blocks: 12 inches square

HOUSE  DRESSING

See the upper Dust Ruffle on the bed underneath the quilt.
Directions are given on page 148.

FABRICS AND SUPPLIES

Yardage is based on 44-inch-wide fabric.

- ♦ ⅔ yard green print fabric for House, Leaf, and Pinwheel Blocks

- ♦ ⅞ yard gold print fabric for Star and Starburst Blocks, pinwheel section, and house windows

- ♦ 1⅛ yards blue print #1 fabric for House and Pinwheel Blocks and middle border

- ♦ 1 yard blue print #2 fabric for House, Pinwheel, and Starburst Blocks

- ♦ ¾ yard red print #1 fabric for House, Leaf, and Pinwheel Blocks

- ♦ 1¼ yards red print #2 fabric for Pinwheel and Starburst Blocks and outer border

- ♦ ¾ yard red print #3 fabric for House, Leaf, and Pinwheel Blocks

- ♦ ⅓ yard chestnut print fabric for Leaf Blocks

- ♦ 1½ yards black print fabric for roof, Checkerboard Sections, and inner border

- ♦ 3⅝ yards beige print fabric for background

- ♦ ⅞ yard red print #2 fabric for binding

- ♦ 5¾ yards fabric for quilt backing

- ♦ Quilt batting, at least 76 × 100 inches

- ♦ Rotary cutter, mat, and wide see-through ruler with ⅛-inch markings

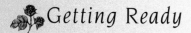

Getting Ready

- Read instructions thoroughly before you begin.

- Prewash and press fabric.

- Place right sides of fabric pieces together and use ¼-inch seam allowances throughout unless directions specify otherwise.

- Seam allowances are included in the cutting sizes given.

- Press seam allowances in the direction that will create the least bulk, and whenever possible, press toward the darker fabric. Press border seam allowances toward the borders unless directions specify otherwise.

- Cutting directions for each section of the quilt are given individually. If you like to cut as you go, simply follow the directions as you get to them. If you'd rather cut all your pieces at the same time, skip ahead to find each of the cutting sections and do all the cutting before you begin.

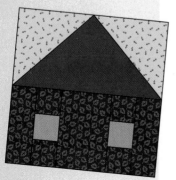

Green | Gold | Blue #1 | Blue #2 | Red #1

Red #2 | Red #3 | Chestnut | Black | Beige

HOUSE BLOCKS

(Make 5)

Cutting

From each of the green, blue #1, blue #2, red #1, and red #3 print fabrics:

- Cut two 2½ × 6-inch strips

- Cut two 2½ × 6½-inch rectangles

- Cut one 4½ × 6½-inch rectangle

From the gold print fabric:

- Cut five 2½ × 6-inch strips

From the beige fabric:

- Cut two 6½ × 44-inch strips. From these strips, cut ten 6½-inch squares.

From the black print fabric:

- Cut two 6½ × 44-inch strips. From these strips, cut five 6½ × 12½-inch rectangles.

Piecing

1 For the green House Block, sew a 2½ × 6-inch green strip to each side of a 2½ × 6-inch gold strip, as shown in **Diagram 1,** and press. Cut two 2½-inch wide segments from this strip set, as shown.

2½"

Diagram 1

2 Sew a Step 1 segment to both sides of the 4½ × 6½-inch green rectangle, as shown in **Diagram 2,** and press. Add the 2½ × 6½-inch green rectangles to the sides of this house unit, as shown, and press.

Diagram 2

Plan Ahead

Here's an easy way to organize and plan for efficient piecing for quilts like Thimbleberries Mix that contain several different blocks and units. Keep a small wooden ladder or drying rack near your sewing area, and hang fabrics that are prewashed, pressed, and ready for stitching on it. This will keep your fabrics wrinkle-free and ready to use at a moment's notice. You can also keep different pieced units, sections, and blocks organized and within easy reach when you are ready to assemble the quilt top.

3 For the blue #1, blue #2, red #1, and red #3 house units, repeat Steps 1 and 2.

4 To make the roof for each house unit, position a 6½-inch beige square on the left corner of each 6½ × 12½-inch black rectangle, as shown at the top of **Diagram 3.** Draw a diagonal line on the beige square, as shown, and stitch on this line. Trim away the excess fabric, leaving a ¼-inch seam allowance, and press, as shown at the middle of the diagram.

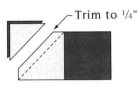

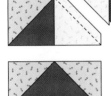

Diagram 3

5 Position a 6½-inch beige square on the opposite corner of each black rectangle, as shown in **Diagram 3.** Draw a diagonal line on the beige square, as shown, and stitch on this line. Trim away the excess fabric as before, and press, as shown at the bottom.

6 Sew the roofs and the house units together, as shown in **Diagram 4,** and press. Make a total of five House Blocks. At this point, the House Blocks should measure 12½ inches square.

Diagram 4

STAR BLOCKS
(Make 5)

Cutting

From the gold print fabric:
- ✦ Cut three 2½ × 44-inch strips. From these strips, cut ten 2½ × 6½-inch rectangles and twenty 2½-inch squares.

From the beige print fabric:
- ✦ Cut five 2½ × 44-inch strips. From these strips, cut twenty 2½ × 4½-inch rectangles and forty 2½-inch squares.

- ✦ Cut two 6½ × 44-inch strips. From these strips, cut ten 6½-inch squares.

Piecing

1 Position a 2½-inch beige square on each corner of the 2½ × 6½-inch gold rectangles, as shown at left in **Diagram 5.** Draw diagonal lines on the beige squares, as shown, and stitch on these lines. Trim away the excess fabric, leaving a ¼-inch seam allowance, and press, as shown at right. Make a total of 10 of these units.

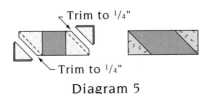

Diagram 5

2 Position a 2½-inch gold square on the right corner of each of the 2½ × 4½-inch beige rectangles, as shown at top left in **Diagram 6.** Draw a diagonal line on each gold square, as shown, and stitch on this line. Trim away the excess fabric, leaving a ¼-inch seam allowance, and press, as shown at top right. Add a 2½-inch beige square to each of these units, as shown at the bottom of the diagram, and press. Make a total of 20 of these units.

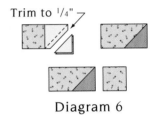

Diagram 6

3 Sew a Step 2 unit to the top and bottom of the Step 1 units, as shown in **Diagram 7,** and press. Make a total of 10 of these star units. At this point, the star units should measure 6½ inches square.

Diagram 7

4 Sew the star units and the 6½-inch beige squares together in pairs, as shown at the top of **Diagram 8** on page 144, and press. Sew these units together in pairs, as shown at the bottom of the diagram. Make a total of five Star Blocks. At this point, the Star Blocks should measure 12½ inches square.

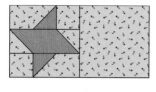

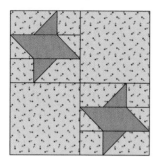

Diagram 8

LEAF BLOCKS
(Make 4)

Cutting

From each of the chestnut, green, red #1, and red #3 print fabrics:

+ Cut one 6½-inch square

+ Cut one 3⅞ × 22-inch strip

+ Cut one 1¼ × 6-inch strip

From the beige print fabric:

+ Cut four 3½-inch squares

+ Cut four 3⅞ × 22-inch strips

+ Cut four more 3½-inch squares. Cut these squares in half diagonally.

Piecing

1 For the chestnut Leaf Block, layer the 3⅞ × 22-inch chestnut and a beige strip together, as shown in **Diagram 9**. Press them together, but do not sew. Cut the layered strips into five 3⅞-inch squares, as shown,

taking care not to shift the layers as you cut.

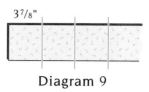

Diagram 9

2 Cut the squares in half diagonally, as shown in **Diagram 10**. Stitch ¼ inch from the diagonal edges, as shown, and press. Make a total of 10 of these triangle-pieced squares. At this point, the triangle-pieced squares should measure 3½ inches square.

Diagram 10

3 For the green, red #1, and red #3 Leaf Blocks, repeat Steps 1 and 2, using the corresponding 3⅞ × 22-inch strips and the 3⅞ × 22-inch beige strips.

4 To make the chestnut stem unit, center a 3½-inch beige triangle on the 1¼ × 6-inch chestnut strip, as shown at top left in **Diagram 11.** Stitch a ¼-inch seam, as shown, and press. Repeat on the other side of the chestnut strip, as shown at top right in the diagram. Press these seam allowances toward the stem. Square off the stem unit to 3½ inches square, making sure the stem is centered, as shown at lower right in the diagram.

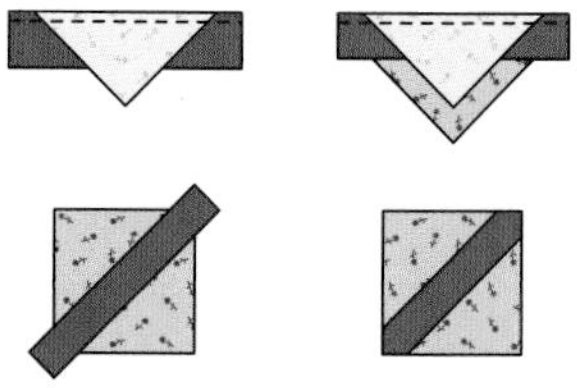

Diagram 11

5 To make the green, red #1, and red #3 stem units, repeat Step 4, using the remaining 3½-inch beige triangles and the corresponding 1¼ × 6-inch strips.

6 The chestnut Leaf Block contains one stem unit, one 3½-inch beige square, one 6½-inch chestnut square, and ten 3½-inch chestnut and beige triangle-pieced squares. Referring to **Diagram 12**, sew the blocks together in rows, and press. At this point, the chestnut Leaf Block should measure 12½ inches square.

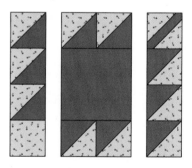

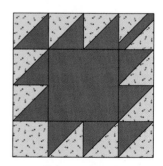

Diagram 12

7 To complete the green, red #1, and red #3 Leaf Blocks, repeat Step 6, using the corresponding fabrics. At this point, these Leaf Blocks should measure 12½ inches square.

Starburst Blocks

(Make 6)

Cutting

From the gold print fabric:
+ Cut one 4½ × 44-inch strip. From this strip, cut six 4½-inch squares.

From the blue print #2 fabric:
+ Cut six 2½ × 44-inch strips. From these strips, cut ninety-six 2½-inch squares.

From the red print #2 fabric:
+ Cut three 2½ × 44-inch strips. From these strips, cut twenty-four 2½ × 4½-inch rectangles.

From the beige print fabric:
+ Cut three 4½ × 44-inch strips. From these strips, cut twenty-four 4½-inch squares.

+ Cut three 2½ × 44-inch strips. From these strips, cut twenty-four 2½ × 4½-inch rectangles.

Piecing

1 Position a 2½-inch blue square on the corner of a 2½ × 4½-inch red rectangle, as shown at top left in **Diagram 13.** Stitch diagonally on the blue square, as shown. Trim the seam allowance to ¼ inch, and press, as shown at top right. Repeat this process at the opposite corner of the red rectangle, as shown at the bottom of the diagram. Make a total of 24 of these star point units.

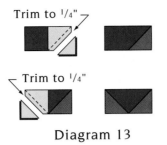
Trim to ¼"
Trim to ¼"

Diagram 13

2 In the same manner, position and sew 2½-inch blue squares on the corners of the 2½ × 4½-inch beige rectangles, as shown in **Diagram 14.** Make a total of 24 of these star point units.

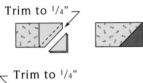
Trim to ¼"
Trim to ¼"

Diagram 14

3 Sew the Step 1 and 2 star point units together in pairs, positioning the Step 2 units on top, as shown in **Diagram 15.**

Diagram 15

4 Sew the Step 3 units to the top and bottom of the 4½-inch gold squares, as shown in **Diagram 16,** and press.

Diagram 16

5 Sew 4½-inch beige squares to both sides of the remaining Step 3 units, as shown in **Diagram 17,** and press. Sew these units to both sides of the Step 4 units, as shown, and press. At this point, the Starburst Blocks should measure 12½ inches square.

Diagram 17

Checkerboard Sections

(Make 2)

Cutting

From the beige print fabric:
+ Cut six 2½ × 44-inch strips

From the black print fabric:
+ Cut six 2½ × 44-inch strips

Piecing

1 Sew 2½ × 44-inch black strips to both sides of two of the 2½ × 44-inch beige strips, as shown in **Diagram 18** on page 146, and press. Make two of Strip Set I, and cross cut them into thirty 2½-inch segments, as shown.

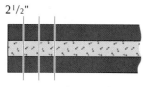

2½"

Strip Set I
Diagram 18

2 Sew 2½ × 44-inch beige strips to both sides of two of the 2½ × 44-inch black strips, as shown in **Diagram 19,** and press. Make two of Strip Set II, and cross cut them into thirty 2½-inch segments, as shown.

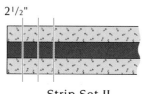

2½"

Strip Set II
Diagram 19

3 Sew 15 Step 1 and 15 Step 2 segments together, alternating colors, as shown in **Diagram 20,** and press. Make two of these Checkerboard Sections. At this point, the Checkerboard Sections should measure 6½ × 60½ inches.

PINWHEEL BLOCKS
(Make 24)

Cutting

From each of the green, red #1, red #2, red #3, blue #1, and blue #2 print fabrics:

◆ Cut one 3⅞ × 44-inch strip

From the beige print fabric:

◆ Cut six 3⅞ × 44-inch strips

◆ Cut two 6½ × 44-inch strips. From these strips, cut twelve 6½-inch squares.

From the gold print fabric:

◆ Cut four 6½-inch squares

Piecing

1 Layer the green 3⅞ × 44-inch strip and a beige strip together, as shown in **Diagram 21.** Press them together, but do not sew. Cut eight 3⅞-inch squares, as shown, taking care not to shift the layers as you cut.

3⅞"

Diagram 21

2 Cut the squares in half diagonally, as shown in **Diagram 22.** Stitch ¼ inch from the diagonal edges, and press. At this point, the 16 triangle-pieced squares should measure 3½ inches square.

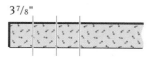

Diagram 22

3 Sew the triangle-pieced squares together in pairs, as shown at left in **Diagram 23.** Sew two pairs of triangle-pieced squares together to form a

Pinwheel Block, as shown at right in the diagram. Repeat this process to make three more green and beige Pinwheel Blocks.

Diagram 23

4 To make the remaining Pinwheel Blocks, repeat Steps 1, 2, and 3, combining the remaining beige strips with the red #1, red #2, red #3, blue #1, and blue #2 strips. At this point, the Pinwheel Blocks should measure 6½ inches square.

5 Referring to the top of the **Quilt Diagram** on page 147 for color placement, sew together twelve Pinwheel Blocks, six 6½-inch beige squares, and two 6½-inch gold squares, and press. Make another Pinwheel section, referring to the bottom of the diagram for color placement, and press.

QUILT CENTER
Assembly

1 Sew the Star Blocks and the House Blocks together in pairs, referring to the **Quilt Diagram** on page 147 for placement. Sew the Checkerboard Sections to both sides of the House/Star section, and press.

Diagram 20

Quilt Diagram

Attaching the Borders

1 To attach the 2½-inch-wide black inner border strips, refer to page 198 for "Border Instructions."

2 To attach the 2½-inch-wide blue middle border strips, refer to page 198 for "Border Instructions."

3 To attach the 2½-inch-wide red outer border strips, refer to page 198 for "Border Instructions."

PUTTING IT ALL TOGETHER

1 Cut the 5¾-yard length of backing fabric in half crosswise to make two 2⅞-yard lengths. Remove the selvages, and sew the long edges together. Press the seam allowances open. Trim the backing and batting so they are about 4 inches larger than the quilt top.

2 For quilting ideas, see the **Quilting Design Diagram.** See page 201 for detailed marking, layering, and finishing instructions.

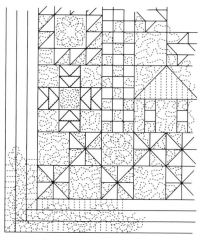

Quilting Design Diagram

2 Sew three Starburst Blocks and two Leaf Blocks together, referring to the **Quilt Diagram,** and press. Make another section like this. Sew these sections to the sides of the quilt center, and press.

3 Sew a Pinwheel section to the top and bottom edges of the quilt, referring to the **Quilt Diagram,** and press.

BORDERS

The yardage given allows for the border strips to be cut on the crosswise grain. The border strips are longer than necessary and will be trimmed later.

Cutting

From the black print fabric:
✦ Cut eight 2½ × 44-inch strips for the inner border

From the blue print #1 fabric:
✦ Cut eight 2½ × 44-inch strips for the middle border

From the red print #2 fabric:
✦ Cut nine 2½ × 44-inch strips for the outer border

BINDING

The 2¾-inch binding strips will produce a ½-inch-wide finished binding. If you want a wider or narrower binding, adjust the width of the strips you cut. (See page 201 for pointers on how to experiment with binding width.) Refer to "Attaching Binding with Mitered Corners" on page 202 to complete your quilt.

Cutting Crosswise Strips

From the red print #2 binding fabric:

✦ Cut nine 2¾ × 44-inch strips on the crosswise grain

HOUSE DRESSING

Dust Ruffle

FABRICS AND SUPPLIES

✦ 60-inch tape measure (A builder's retractable metal tape measure is very helpful for measuring beds.)

✦ Muslin for attaching dust ruffle and covering surface of box spring

✦ Fabric for dust ruffle (Determine the yardage for your dust ruffle by measuring the size of your bed, as indicated in the instructions below.)

✦ Sewing machine

✦ Thread to match fabric of dust ruffle

✦ One spool #8 DMC pearl cotton (or two strands of quilting thread for gathering top edge of dust ruffle)

✦ 6 × 24-inch-wide see-through ruler with ⅛-inch markings

✦ Rotary cutter and mat

1 Measure the box spring of your bed without the mattress in place. The dust ruffle will be attached to a center panel that fits over the box spring, and the weight of the mattress will hold it in place.

2 Cut a center panel of muslin to fit the top of your box spring, allowing ½-inch seam allowance on the sides and the lower edge, and adding 2¼ inches across the top, to allow for hemming. Join widths of fabric together, if necessary.

3 To hem the top edge of the center panel, turn the top edge under ¼ inch, and press. Turn under 2 more inches, and press again. Topstitch the folded edge in place, as shown in **Diagram 1.**

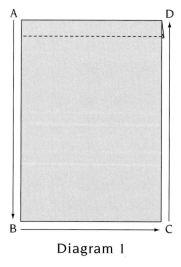

Diagram 1

4 To determine the correct drop length for your dust ruffle, measure from the top edge of your box spring to the floor, and add 2½ inches to allow for a hem and seam allowances.

5 To determine the number of fabric strips to cut for your dust ruffle, measure around your center panel from point A to points B, C, and D, as shown in **Diagram 1** on page 148. Multiply this measurement by 2.5 to 3, depending on the weight of your fabric and the amount of fullness you want in your dust ruffle. Cut as many strips of fabric as needed to equal this length. The width of each strip should be the measurement determined in Step 4. Sew the short ends of these strips together, and press the seam allowances open. Press and stitch a 1-inch double-fold hem along one long edge, for the bottom of the dust ruffle.

6 Divide the edge of the dust ruffle into fourths, and mark the quarter points with straight pins. To gather the top edge of the dust ruffle, position the length of pearl cotton ¼ inch in from the raw edge of the fabric. The length of this pearl cotton should be one and a half times the circumference of your bed. Stitch across one end of it to secure it in place, as shown in **Diagram 2.** Start to zigzag stitch over the pearl cotton, taking care not to sew through it as you go. Hold onto the pearl cotton, pushing the fabric so it will gather as you continue stitching.

Diagram 2

7 Divide the muslin center panel into fourths from point A to D, and mark these quarter points with pins. Lay the dust ruffle right side down on top of the muslin center panel, matching quarter points marked by pins, as shown in **Diagram 3.** Pin the gathered edge to the center panel, as shown. Pull on the pearl cotton, gathering the dust ruffle evenly to fit. Pin and stitch the dust ruffle to the center panel, using a ½-inch seam allowance.

NOTE: *See pages 23, 77, 172, and 180 for other dust ruffles made in the same manner.*

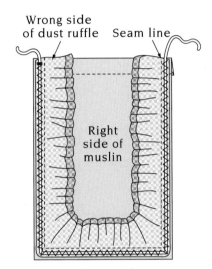

Diagram 3

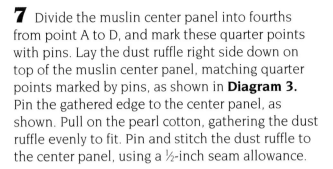

SHINING STAR

MAKE IT IN A WEEKEND

SIZE

Wall Quilt: 34 inches square (unquilted)

FABRICS AND SUPPLIES

Yardage is based on 44-inch-wide fabric.

◆ ⅓ yard gold print #1 fabric for Star Block

◆ ⅞ yard gold print #2 fabric for Star Block background, inner border, and corner squares

◆ ⅔ yard beige print fabric for background and corner triangle blocks

◆ ½ yard blue floral fabric for quilt center and corner triangle blocks

◆ ½ yard blue plaid fabric for outer border

◆ ½ yard blue floral fabric for binding

◆ 1⅛ yards fabric for quilt backing

◆ Quilt batting, at least 38 inches square

◆ Rotary cutter, mat, and wide see-through ruler with ⅛-inch markings

Color Play

See page 152 for a creative color variation on the quilt shown here.

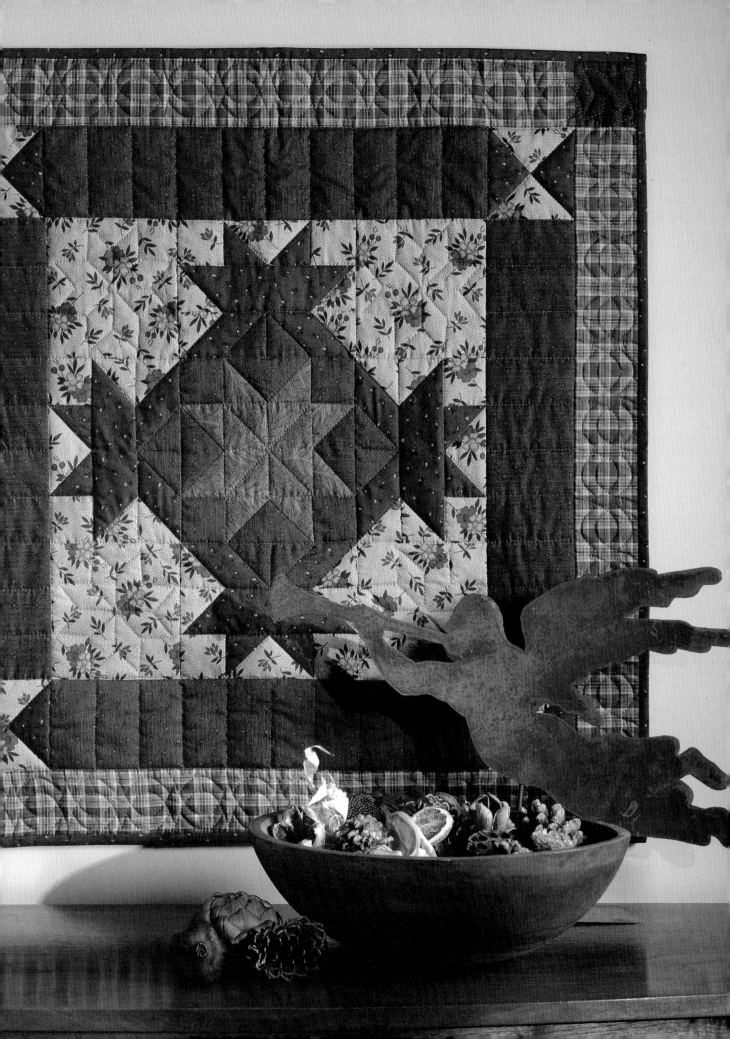

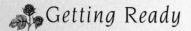

Getting Ready

- Read instructions thoroughly before you begin.

- Prewash and press fabric.

- Place right sides of fabric pieces together and use ¼-inch seam allowances throughout unless directions specify otherwise.

- Seam allowances are included in the cutting sizes given.

- Press seam allowances in the direction that will create the least bulk, and whenever possible, press toward the darker fabric. Press border seam allowances toward the borders unless directions specify otherwise.

- Cutting directions for each section of the quilt are given individually. If you like to cut as you go, simply follow the directions as you get to them. If you'd rather cut all your pieces at the same time, skip ahead to find each of the cutting sections and do all the cutting before you begin.

FABRIC KEY
(for the quilt shown on page 151)

Gold #1	Gold #2	Beige	Blue floral	Blue plaid

Color Play

The deep gold that surrounds the center star in the project quilt on page 151 is also featured in this color variation. Here, a deep shade of red and a lighter background color transform the soft look of the gold and blue stars from casual to dramatic.

SHINING • STAR

STAR BLOCK

(Make 1)

Cutting

From the gold print #1 fabric:

✦ Cut one 4½-inch square

✦ Cut one 2½ × 44-inch strip. From this strip, cut eight 2½-inch squares.

From the gold print #2 fabric:

✦ Cut one 2½ × 44-inch strip. From this strip, cut four 2½ × 4½-inch rectangles and four 2½-inch squares.

Piecing

1 Position a 2½-inch gold #1 square on the corner of a 2½ × 4½-inch gold #2 rectangle, as shown at the top of **Diagram 1.** Stitch diagonally from corner to corner on the gold #1 square, as shown. Trim the seam allowance to ¼ inch and press, as shown at upper right. Repeat this process at the opposite corner of the gold #2 rectangle, as shown at the bottom of the diagram. Make a total of four of these star point units.

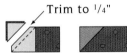
Trim to ¼"

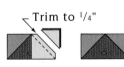
Trim to ¼"

Diagram 1

2 Sew a star point unit to the top and to the bottom of the 4½-inch gold #1 square, as shown in **Diagram 2,** and press.

Diagram 2

3 Sew a 2½-inch gold #2 square to each end of the remaining star point units, as shown in **Diagram 3,** and press.

Diagram 3

4 Sew these Step 3 units to both sides of the Star Block, as shown in **Diagram 4,** and press. At this point, the Star Block should measure 8½ inches square.

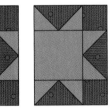

Diagram 4

QUILT CENTER

Cutting

From the blue floral fabric:

✦ Cut three 2½ × 44-inch strips. From these strips, cut four 2½ × 8½-inch rectangles, eight 2½ × 4½-inch rectangles, and eight 2½-inch squares.

From the beige print fabric:

✦ Cut two 2½ × 44-inch strips. From these strips, cut four 2½ × 4½-inch rectangles and twenty-four 2½-inch squares.

✦ Cut four 6½-inch squares

From the gold print #2 fabric:

✦ Cut one 2½ × 44-inch strip. From this strip, cut eight 2½-inch squares.

Piecing

1 Position a 2½-inch blue floral square on the corner of a 2½ × 4½-inch beige rectangle, as shown at top left in **Diagram 5.** Stitch diagonally from corner to corner on the blue floral square, as shown. Trim the seam allowance to ¼ inch, and press, as shown at top right. Repeat this process at the opposite corner of the beige rectangle, as shown in the middle part of the diagram. Sew a 2½-inch beige square to both sides of these units, as shown at the bottom of the diagram, and press. Make a total of four of these units.

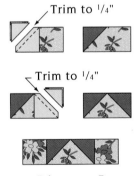
Trim to ¼"

Trim to ¼"

Diagram 5

2 Position a 2½-inch beige square on each corner of the 2½ × 8½-inch blue floral rectangles, as shown at the top of **Diagram 6** on page 154. Stitch diagonally from corner to corner on the beige squares, as shown.

Trim the seam allowances to ¼ inch, and press, as shown at the bottom of the diagram. Make a total of four of these units.

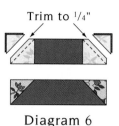

Diagram 6

3 Position a 2½-inch beige square on the left corner of a 2½ × 4½-inch blue floral rectangle, as shown at top left in **Diagram 7.** Stitch diagonally from corner to corner on the beige square, as shown. Trim the seam allowance to ¼ inch and press, as shown at top right. Position a 2½-inch gold square on the right corner of this rectangle, as shown at bottom left. Stitch diagonally from corner to corner on the gold square, as shown. Trim the seam allowance to ¼ inch and press, as shown at bottom right. Make a total of four of these units.

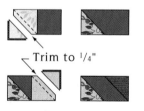

Diagram 7

4 Referring to **Diagram 8,** position a 2½-inch beige square on the right corner of a 2½ × 4½-inch blue floral rectangle, as shown at top left in the diagram. Stitch, trim, and press the unit in the same manner as in Step 3. Position a 2½-inch gold square on the left corner of this rectangle, as shown at the

bottom of the diagram. Stitch, trim, and press the unit in the same fashion as instructed in Step 3. Make a total of four of these units.

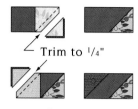

Diagram 8

5 Sew the Step 3 and Step 4 units together in pairs, as shown in **Diagram 9,** and press.

Diagram 9

6 Referring to **Diagram 10,** sew Step 1, Step 2, and Step 5 units together, and press. Make a total of four of these units. At this point, the units

should measure 6½ × 8½ inches.

Diagram 10

7 Sew Step 6 units to the top and bottom of the Star Block, referring to the **Quilt Diagram,** and press.

8 Sew 6½-inch beige squares to the remaining Step 6 units, and press. Sew these units to the sides of the Star Block, referring to the **Quilt Diagram.**

BORDERS

The yardage given allows for the inner border strips, outer border strips, and corner squares to be cut on the crosswise grain. The border strips are longer than necessary and will be trimmed later.

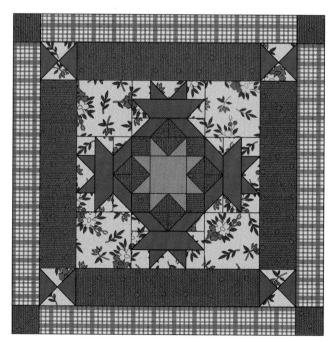

Quilt Diagram

Cutting

From the gold print #2 fabric:

◆ Cut two 4½ × 44-inch strips for the inner border

◆ Cut four 3½-inch corner squares

From the beige print fabric:

◆ Cut two 5¼-inch squares. Cut the squares diagonally into quarters, forming eight triangles.

From the blue floral fabric:

◆ Cut two 5¼-inch squares. Cut the squares diagonally into quarters, forming eight triangles.

From the blue plaid fabric:

◆ Cut four 3½ × 30-inch strips for the outer border

After cutting the border strips for Shining Star, save any leftover pieces or strips of fabric, and start a collection of leftover border strips in varying widths. They can be used to piece together an interesting backing for another small quilt.

Piecing

1 To make the corner triangle blocks, layer a blue floral triangle on a beige triangle, as shown in **Diagram 11.** Sew a ¼-inch seam along one of the bias edges, as shown, being careful not to stretch the triangles. Repeat for the remaining blue floral and beige triangles. Make sure you sew with the blue floral fabric on top, and along the same bias edge of each triangle set, so that your pieced triangle units will all have the blue triangle on the same side.

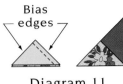

Diagram 11

2 Sew the Step 1 triangle units together in pairs to make the corner triangle blocks, as shown in **Diagram 12,** and press. At this point, the corner triangle blocks should measure 4½ inches square.

Diagram 12

3 To attach the 4½-inch-wide gold top and bottom border strips, as shown in the **Quilt Diagram** on page 154, refer to page 198 for "Border Instructions."

4 To attach the 4½-inch-wide gold side border strips with corner triangle blocks, as shown in the **Quilt Diagram,** refer to page 200 for "Borders with Corner Squares."

5 To attach the 3½-inch-wide blue plaid top and bottom border strips, as shown in the **Quilt Diagram,** refer to page 198 for "Border Instructions."

6 To attach the 3½-inch-wide blue plaid side border strips with gold corner squares, as shown in the **Quilt Diagram,** refer to page 200 for "Borders with Corner Squares."

PUTTING IT ALL TOGETHER

1 Trim the backing and batting so they are about 4 inches larger than the quilt top.

2 For quilting ideas, see the **Quilting Design Diagram.** See page 201 for detailed marking, layering, and finishing instructions.

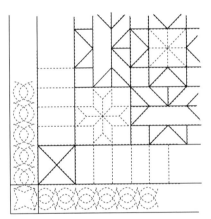

Quilting Design Diagram

BINDING

The 2¾-inch binding strips will produce a ½-inch-wide finished binding. If you want a wider or narrower binding, adjust the width of the strips you cut. (See page 201 for pointers on how to experiment with binding width.) Refer to "Attaching Binding with Mitered Corners" on page 202 to complete your quilt.

Cutting Crosswise Strips

From the blue floral binding fabric:

◆ Cut four 2¾ × 44-inch strips on the crosswise grain

A PATCH
OF PUMPKINS

MAKE
IT
TONIGHT

SIZE

Wall Quilt: 24 × 28 inches (unquilted)

HOUSE
DRESSING

See the Papier-Mâché Box on the trunk below the quilt.
Directions are given on page 163.

FABRICS AND SUPPLIES

Yardage is based on 44-inch-wide fabric.

+ ⅛ yard each of orange print #1, green print #2, and russet print fabric for Patchwork Section and binding

+ ⅛ yard green print #1 fabric for Patchwork Section and leaf appliqués

+ ¼ yard beige print fabric for Fence

+ ¼ yard orange print #2 fabric for pumpkin appliqués

+ ⅜ yard black print fabric for Patchwork Section, Background, corner squares, appliqués, and binding

+ ¼ yard gold print fabric for inner border and star appliqués

+ ½ yard brown check fabric for Patchwork Section and outer border

+ ¼ yard paper-backed fusible web

+ One spool each #8 DMC black and gold pearl cotton

+ ⅓ yard fabric for binding (or use scraps for multicolored binding, as indicated in the instructions)

+ ⅞ yard fabric for quilt backing

+ Quilt batting, at least 28 × 32 inches

+ Rotary cutter, mat, and wide see-through ruler with ⅛-inch markings

156

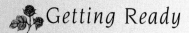

- Orange #1
- Orange #2
- Green #1
- Green #2
- Russet
- Beige
- Black
- Gold
- Brown check

✿ Read instructions thoroughly before you begin.

✿ Note that the appliqué in this project is done using the fusible appliqué method.

✿ Prewash and press fabric.

✿ Place right sides of fabric pieces together and use ¼-inch seam allowances throughout unless directions specify otherwise.

✿ Seam allowances are included in the cutting sizes given.

✿ Press seam allowances in the direction that will create the least bulk, and whenever possible, press toward the darker fabric. Press border seam allowances toward the borders unless directions specify otherwise.

✿ Cutting directions for each section of the quilt are given individually. If you like to cut as you go, simply follow the directions as you get to them. If you'd rather cut all your pieces at the same time, skip ahead to find each of the cutting sections and do all the cutting before you begin.

TRIANGLE-PIECED SQUARES

(Make 8)

Cutting

From the orange print #1 fabric:
- ✦ Cut one 2⅞ × 14-inch strip

From the green print #1 fabric:
- ✦ Cut one 2⅞ × 14-inch strip

Piecing

1 Layer the 2⅞ × 14-inch orange and green strips right sides together. Press them together, but do not sew. Cut the layered strips into four 2⅞-inch squares.

2 Cut the layered squares in half diagonally. Stitch ¼ inch away from the diagonal edge, as shown in **Diagram 1,** and press. Make a total of eight of these Triangle-Pieced Squares. At this time, the Triangle-Pieced Squares should measure 2½ inches square.

Diagram 1

PATCHWORK SECTION

Cutting

From the orange print #1 fabric:
- ✦ Cut one 2½-inch square

From the green print #2 fabric:
- ✦ Cut one 2½ × 15-inch strip. From this strip, cut five 2½-inch squares.

From the russet print fabric:
- ✦ Cut one 2½ × 12-inch strip. From this strip, cut four 2½-inch squares.

From the green print #1 fabric:
- ✦ Cut one 2½ × 12-inch strip. From this strip, cut four 2½-inch squares.

From the black print fabric:
- ✦ Cut one 2½ × 27-inch strip. From this strip, cut ten 2½-inch squares.

From the brown check fabric:
- ✦ Cut one 2½ × 16½-inch rectangle

Piecing

Referring to the **Quilt Diagram** on page 159 for color placement, sew the squares and Triangle-Pieced Squares together in horizontal rows, and press. Sew the horizontal rows and the 2½ × 16½-inch brown check rectangle together, and press. Two of the Triangle-Pieced Squares will lie underneath the lower pumpkin appliqué.

FENCE AND BACKGROUND

Cutting

From the black print fabric:
✦ Cut one 4½ × 16½-inch rectangle

✦ Cut one 2½ × 22-inch strip. From this strip, cut eight 2½-inch squares.

From the beige print fabric:
✦ Cut two 2½ × 44-inch strips. From these strips, cut eight 2½ × 6½-inch rectangles.

Piecing

1 Position a 2½-inch black square on the corner of each 2½ × 6½-inch beige rectangle, as shown in **Diagram 2.** Stitch diagonally from corner to corner on the black square, as shown. Trim the seam allowance to ¼ inch, and press. Make a total of eight fence posts.

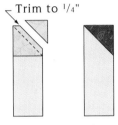

Diagram 2

2 Sew the fence posts together in a row, referring to the **Quilt Diagram,** and press. Sew the 4½ × 16½-inch black rec-

tangle to the top of the fence section, as shown, and press.

3 Referring to the **Quilt Diagram,** sew the fence section to the top of the Patchwork Section, and press.

BORDERS

The yardage given allows for the border strips to be cut on the crosswise grain. The border strips are longer than necessary and will be trimmed later.

Cutting

From the gold print fabric:
✦ Cut two 1½ × 44-inch strips for the inner border

From the brown check fabric:
✦ Cut three 3½ × 44-inch strips for the outer border

From the black print fabric:
✦ Cut four 3½-inch corner squares

Attaching the Borders

1 To attach the 1½-inch-wide gold inner border strips, as shown in the **Quilt Diagram,** refer to page 198 for "Border Instructions."

2 To attach the 3½-inch-wide brown check top and bottom outer border strips, as shown in the **Quilt Diagram,** refer to page 198 for "Border Instructions."

3 To attach the 3½-inch-wide brown check side outer border strips with black corner squares, as shown in the **Quilt Diagram,** refer to page 200 for "Borders with Corner Squares."

Quilt Diagram

APPLIQUÉING

Some of the appliqué pattern pieces on page 162 are reversed for tracing purposes, so they will appear in the correct positions when stitched. Follow the tracing instructions provided on each pattern piece.

1 Position the fusible web (paper side up) over the appliqué shapes on pages 161–162. Trace three A Pumpkins, three B Leaves, four C Stars, one each of D, E, and F Mouths, two of G Eyes, a total of four H for Noses and Eyes, and a total of three I for Nose and Eyes, leaving at least ½ inch between each shape.

2 Roughly cut around the traced shapes, as shown in **Diagram 3.**

NOTE: *When you are fusing a large shape, like the A Pumpkin, fuse just the outer edges of the shape, so that it will not look stiff when finished. To do this, draw a line about ⅜ inch inside the pumpkin, and cut away the fusible web on this line, as shown.*

Diagram 3

3 Following the manufacturer's instructions, fuse the shapes to the wrong side of the fabrics you have selected, as shown in **Diagram 4.** Let the fabric cool, and cut along the outline of each shape, as shown. Peel away the paper from the fusible web.

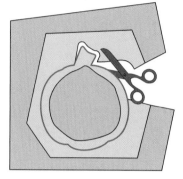

Diagram 4

4 Referring to the photographed quilt on page 157 for placement, position and fuse the A Pumpkin shapes on the wall quilt, followed by shapes B, C, D, E, F, G, H, and I.

5 Using the buttonhole stitch and one strand of black pearl cotton, appliqué the stars, pumpkins, eyes, noses, and mouths in place. Appliqué the leaves using the buttonhole stitch and one strand of gold pearl cotton. Refer to page 197 for "Decorative Stitches."

PUTTING IT ALL TOGETHER

1 Trim the backing and batting so they are about 4 inches larger than the quilt top.

2 For quilting ideas, see the **Quilting Design Diagram.** See page 201 for detailed marking, layering, and finishing instructions.

Quilting Design Diagram

When you're ready to cut strips of fabric for the multicolored pieced binding for A Patch of Pumpkins, you can also take the opportunity to start a collection of 2¾-inch-wide strips in varying lengths for use in future quilts. Cut a few extra strips in each of the four fabrics for the binding of this quilt, and store them together in a plastic bag marked with the words Binding Strips. Add more strips to it whenever you can, and you'll always have a colorful stash of strips to choose from for pieced bindings.

Binding

The 2¾-inch binding strips will produce a ½-inch-wide finished binding. If you want a wider or narrower binding, adjust the width of the strips you cut. (See page 201 for pointers on how to experiment with binding width.) Refer to "Attaching Binding with Mitered Corners" on page 202 to complete your quilt.

Cutting Crosswise Strips

From each of the black, russet, orange #1, and green #2 print fabrics:

✦ Cut two 2¾ × 14-inch strips on the crosswise grain

or

From one binding fabric:

✦ Cut three 2¾ × 44-inch strips on the crosswise grain

A
Pumpkin
(TRACE 3)

This appliqué shape is reversed for tracing purposes.
It will appear in the correct position when traced onto fusible web.

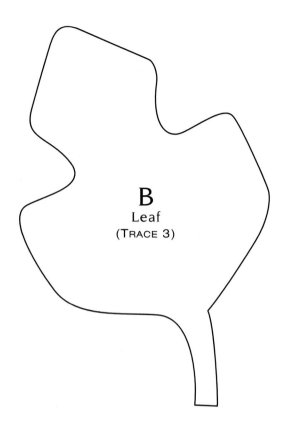

B
Leaf
(TRACE 3)

C
Star
(TRACE 4)

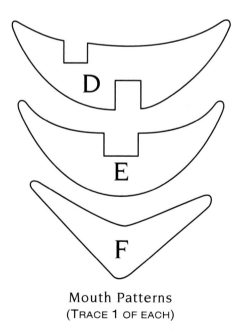

D

E

F

Mouth Patterns
(TRACE 1 OF EACH)

G
Eye

(TRACE 1 AND 1 REVERSED)

H

TRACE 2 FOR NOSES
TRACE 2 FOR EYES

I

TRACE 2 FOR EYES
TRACE 1 FOR NOSE

HOUSE DRESSING

Papier-Mâché Box

SUPPLIES

All supplies are available from hobby or craft stores.

+ Papier-mâché box with lid (any size or shape)

+ Latex paint for walls

+ Medium sandpaper

+ Appliqué shapes from pages 161–162

+ Template plastic

+ Stencil paints for walls

+ Walnut wood stain (optional)

+ Acrylic matte spray

1 Paint the box and the lid top with any color latex paint you like, and allow the paint to dry for 4 hours. The edges of the lid may be left un-painted to create a contrast, or you can paint them with a different color.

2 To give the box the look of age, use the medium sandpaper to sand off the paint, exposing parts of the surface of the papier-mâché box.

3 To make a stencil, mark the appliqué shapes on pages 161–162 onto template plastic and cut the shapes out of the plastic, exactly on the marked lines.

4 Using stencil paints for walls, stencil the shapes on the box, and allow the paints to dry for 24 hours. For a large box, use pumpkins on the base, and stars and leaves on the lid. If your box is small, put just stars on the base and lid.

5 If desired, sand the stenciled designs lightly to give them an antique look.

6 If desired, use walnut wood stain and a clean, dry rag to rub the stain over the entire surface of the box. Wipe off any excess stain, and allow it to dry for 24 hours.

7 To seal the surface of the box, spray it with acrylic matte finish.

PICNIC TABLE RUNNER

SIZE

Table Runner: 26 × 44 inches (unquilted)

 ## HOUSE DRESSING

See the Appliquéd Tablecloth on the table under the runner. Directions are given on page 169.

FABRICS AND SUPPLIES

Yardage is based on 44-inch-wide fabric.

+ ⅝ yard red print fabric for Checkerboard Center, Nine Patch Blocks, and middle border

+ ⅝ yard beige print fabric for Checkerboard Center and fence

+ ⅓ yard green print #1 fabric for Nine Patch Blocks and fence background

+ ⅓ yard brown print fabric for inner border

+ ⅜ yard blue print fabric for outer border and flower appliqués

+ ⅛ yard green print #2 fabric for leaf appliqués

+ ½ yard gold print fabric for flower center appliqués and binding

+ ½ yard paper-backed fusible web

+ One spool each #8 DMC black and gold pearl cotton

+ 1⅓ yards fabric for quilt backing

+ Quilt batting, at least 30 × 48 inches

+ Rotary cutter, mat, and wide see-through ruler with ⅛-inch markings

Getting Ready

* Read instructions thoroughly before you begin.

* Note that the appliqué in this project is done using the fusible appliqué method.

* Prewash and press fabric.

* Place right sides of fabric pieces together and use ¼-inch seam allowances throughout unless directions specify otherwise.

* Seam allowances are included in the cutting sizes given.

* Press seam allowances in the direction that will create the least bulk, and whenever possible, press toward the darker fabric. Press border seam allowances toward the borders unless directions specify otherwise.

* Cutting directions for each section of the quilt are given individually. If you like to cut as you go, simply follow the directions as you get to them. If you'd rather cut all your pieces at the same time, skip ahead to find each of the cutting sections and do all the cutting before you begin.

Red Beige Green #1

Brown Blue Green #2 Gold

CHECKERBOARD CENTER

Cutting

From the red print fabric:
+ Cut two 2½ × 44-inch strips

From the beige print fabric:
+ Cut two 2½ × 44-inch strips

Piecing

1 Sew the 2½ × 44-inch red and beige strips together in pairs, as shown in **Diagram 1,** and press. Make a total of two of these strip sets, and cross cut them into twenty-six 2½-inch segments, as shown.

2½"

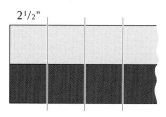

Diagram 1

2 Sew two segments together, alternating colors, as shown at left in **Diagram 2,** and press. Make 13 of these rows, and sew

them together to make the Checkerboard Center, as shown, and press. At this point, the Checkerboard Center should measure 8½ × 26½ inches.

Diagram 2

NINE PATCH BLOCKS
(Make 4)

Cutting

From the red print fabric:
+ Cut one 1½ × 14-inch strip
+ Cut two 1½ × 8-inch strips

From the green print #1 fabric:
+ Cut two 1½ × 14-inch strips
+ Cut one 1½ × 8-inch strip

Piecing

1 Sew a 1½ × 14-inch green strip to each side of the 1½ × 14-inch red strip to make Strip Set I, as shown in **Diagram 3,** and press. Cross cut this strip set into eight 1½-inch segments, as shown.

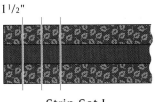

1½"

Strip Set I
Diagram 3

2 Sew a 1½ × 8-inch red strip to each side of the 1½ × 8-inch green strip to form Strip Set II, as shown in **Diagram 4,** and press. Cross cut this strip set into four 1½-inch segments, as shown.

1½"

Strip Set II
Diagram 4

3 Sew a Strip Set I segment to each side of Strip Set II segments, as shown in **Diagram 5,** and press. Make a total of four Nine Patch Blocks. At this point, the Nine Patch Blocks should measure 3½ inches square.

Diagram 5

FENCE SECTIONS

Cutting

From the beige print fabric:
- Cut one 1½ × 44-inch strip
- Cut three 2½ × 44-inch strips. From these strips, cut twenty-four 2½ × 3½-inch rectangles.

From the green print #1 fabric:
- Cut two 1½ × 44-inch strips
- Cut two more 1½ × 44-inch strips. From these strips, cut forty-eight 1½-inch squares.

Piecing

1 Sew the 1½ × 44-inch green strips to each side of the 1½ × 44-inch beige strip, as shown in **Diagram 6,** and press. Cross cut this strip set into twenty 1½-inch segments, as shown.

1½"

Diagram 6

2 Position a 1½-inch green square on the corner of a 2½ × 3½-inch beige rectangle, as shown at top left in **Diagram 7.** Stitch diagonally from corner to corner on the green square, trim the seam allowance to ¼ inch, and press, as shown at top right. Repeat this process at the opposite corner of the beige rectangle, as shown at the bottom of the diagram. Make a total of 24 of these units.

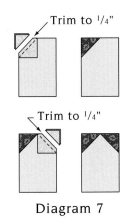

Trim to ¼"

Trim to ¼"

Diagram 7

3 To make a short Fence Section, sew two Step 1 units and three Step 2 units together, referring to the **Quilt Diagram** on page 168, and press. Repeat to make another short Fence Section. Sew these sections to the short ends of the Checkerboard Center, and press.

4 To make a long Fence Section, sew eight Step 1 units and nine Step 2 units together, referring to the **Quilt Diagram,** and press. Repeat to make another long Fence Section, and press. Sew a Nine Patch Block to each end of these Fence Sections, and press. Sew these sections to the sides of the Checkerboard Center, and press.

Plan Ahead

If you decide to appliqué on the Checkerboard Center before adding the borders, do a line of staystitching ¼ inch in from the edges before you start. This will keep the fabric from stretching while you do the buttonhole stitching.

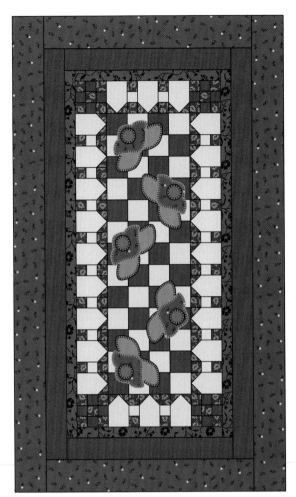

Quilt Diagram

APPLIQUÉING

1 Position the fusible web (paper side up) over the appliqué shapes on page 170. Trace five A Flowers, five B Flower Centers, and ten C Leaves, leaving at least ½ inch between each shape.

2 Roughly cut out the pieces outside your traced lines, as shown in **Diagram 8.**

NOTE: *When you are fusing a large shape, like the A Flower, fuse just the outer edges of the shape, so that it will not look stiff when finished. To do this, draw a line about ⅜ inch inside the flower, and cut away the fusible web on this line, as shown. This will also make it much easier to buttonhole stitch the B Flower Centers later.*

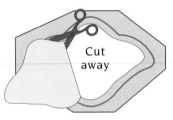

Diagram 8

BORDERS

The yardage given allows for the border strips to be cut on the crosswise grain. The border strips are longer than necessary and will be trimmed later.

Cutting

From the brown print fabric:
+ Cut three 1½ × 44-inch strips for the inner border

From the red print fabric:
+ Cut three 2½ × 44-inch strips for the middle border

From the blue print fabric:
+ Cut four 3½ × 44-inch strips for the outer border

Attaching the Borders

1 To attach the 1½-inch-wide brown inner border strips, as shown in the **Quilt Diagram,** refer to page 198 for "Border Instructions."

2 To attach the 2½-inch-wide red middle border strips, as shown in the **Quilt Diagram,** refer to page 198 for "Border Instructions."

3 To attach the 3½-inch-wide blue outer border strips, as shown in the **Quilt Diagram,** refer to page 198 for "Border Instructions."

3 Following the manufacturer's instructions, fuse the shapes to the wrong side of the fabrics, as shown in **Diagram 9.** Let the fabric cool, and cut along the outline of each shape, as shown. Peel away the paper from the fusible web.

Wrong side of fabric

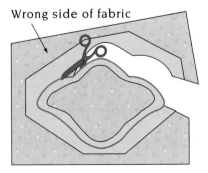

Diagram 9

4 Referring to the **Quilt Diagram** on page 168 for placement, position and fuse the C Leaf shapes on the table runner, followed by the A Flowers and B Flower Centers.

5 Using one strand of gold pearl cotton, appliqué the A Flowers in place by hand with the buttonhole stitch. Using one strand of black pearl cotton, appliqué the B Flower Centers and C Leaves in place. Refer to page 197 for "Decorative Stitches."

PUTTING IT ALL TOGETHER

1 Trim the backing and batting so they are about 4 inches larger than the table runner top.

2 For quilting ideas, see the **Quilting Design Diagram.** See page 201 for detailed marking, layering, and finishing instructions.

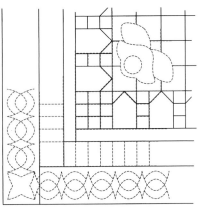

Quilting Design Diagram

BINDING

The 2¾-inch binding strips will produce a ½-inch-wide finished binding. If you want a wider or narrower binding, adjust the width of the strips you cut. (See page 201 for pointers on how to experiment with binding width.) Refer to "Attaching Binding with Mitered Corners" on page 202 to complete your quilt.

Cutting Crosswise Strips

From the gold print binding fabric:
+ Cut four 2¾ × 44-inch strips on the crosswise grain

HOUSE DRESSING
Appliquéd Tablecloth

Finished Tablecloth: 60 × 80 inches

FABRICS AND SUPPLIES

+ 60 × 80-inch piece of checked fabric
+ 2 yards paper-backed fusible web
+ ⅓ yard blue print fabric for flower appliqués
+ ⅛ yard gold print fabric for flower center appliqués
+ ⅓ yard green print fabric for leaf appliqués
+ One spool each #8 DMC black and gold pearl cotton

1 Pull out enough threads along all four edges of the 60 × 80-inch piece of checked fabric to create ½-inch fringe on all sides.

2 Referring to page 168 for appliqué instructions, appliqué three A Flowers and B Flower Centers and six C Leaves from the patterns on page 170 at each corner of the tablecloth, as shown in **Diagram 1.**

Diagram 1

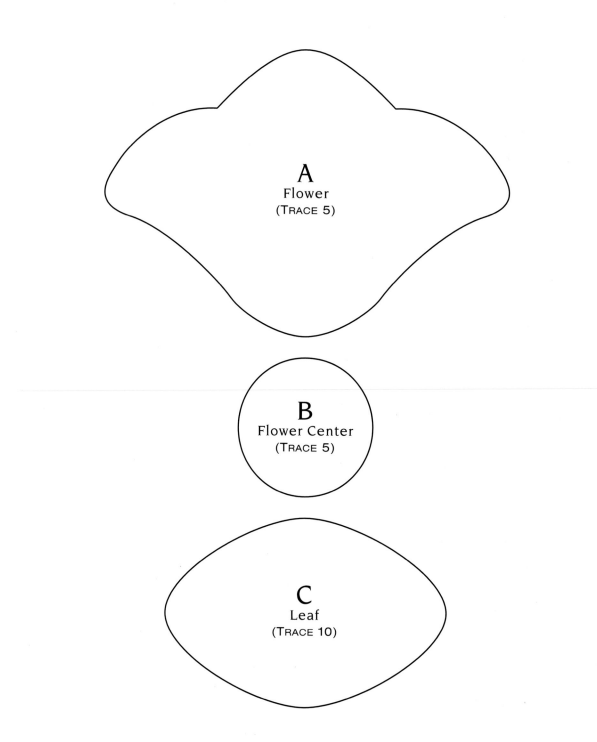

A
Flower
(TRACE 5)

B
Flower Center
(TRACE 5)

C
Leaf
(TRACE 10)

Jamie O'Brien
Law Professor

My Life When I'm Not Quilting

Teaching undergraduate classes in agricultural, labor, and business law, and business finance at South Dakota State University gives me a chance to use both my J.D. law degree and my master's degree in accounting. Plus, my teaching career gives me summers free to enjoy quilting!

Why I Quilt

Quilting is my escape from the world, something I like to do by myself. I don't have a lot of patience, so I try to quilt when I can work without interruption. All of the classes I teach are morning sessions, so whenever I'm all caught up with papers and exams and feel like I can afford an afternoon away from campus, I like to come home and get energized by piecing a quilt.

My Best Tip for Finding More Time for Quilting

Analyze tasks you do routinely and figure out how they can be accomplished in less time. For example, I always keep my children's clothes separated when I do laundry—only one son's clothing goes into my washing machine or dryer at any time. That way, I save the time I would have spent sorting and gain at least 1 or 2 hours for quilting each week.

> *There's nothing better than finishing a quilt and watching your family fight over who gets it.*
>
> —Jamie O'Brien

PINE VALLEY

SIZE

Bed Quilt: 75 × 95 inches (unquilted)
Finished Block: 14 inches square

HOUSE DRESSING

See the Double-Ruffled Pillow Sham on the bed.
Directions are given on page 178.

FABRICS AND SUPPLIES

Yardage is based on 44-inch-wide fabric.

- ◆ 1¾ yards green print fabric for trees

- ◆ ¾ yard brown print fabric for trunks

- ◆ 1⅝ yards wheat print fabric for background

- ◆ ⅓ yard gold print fabric for lattice posts

- ◆ ¾ yard dark green print fabric for inner border

- ◆ 2¼ yards brown check fabric for lattice posts and outer border

- ◆ 1⅞ yards red print fabric for side and corner triangles

- ◆ ¾ yard brown print fabric for binding

- ◆ 5½ yards fabric for quilt backing

- ◆ Quilt batting, at least 79 × 99 inches

- ◆ Rotary cutter, mat, and wide see-through ruler with ⅛-inch markings

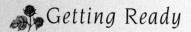

❧ Read instructions thoroughly before you begin.

❧ Prewash and press fabric.

❧ Place right sides of fabric pieces together and use ¼-inch seam allowances throughout unless directions specify otherwise.

❧ Seam allowances are included in the cutting sizes given.

❧ Press seam allowances in the direction that will create the least bulk, and whenever possible, press toward the darker fabric. Press border seam allowances toward the borders unless directions specify otherwise.

❧ Cutting directions for each section of the quilt are given individually. If you like to cut as you go, simply follow the directions as you get to them. If you'd rather cut all your pieces at the same time, skip ahead to find each of the cutting sections and do all the cutting before you begin.

FABRIC KEY

(for the quilt shown on page 173)

- Green
- Brown print
- Wheat
- Gold
- Dark green
- Brown check
- Red

TREE BLOCKS

(Make 18)

Cutting

From the green print fabric:
- ✦ Cut four 8½ × 44-inch strips. From these strips, cut eighteen 8½-inch squares.

- ✦ Cut six 2½ × 44-inch strips. From these strips, cut thirty-six 2½ × 6½-inch rectangles.

From the brown print fabric:
- ✦ Cut two 2½ × 44-inch strips. From these strips, cut eighteen 2½-inch squares.

- ✦ Cut one 2⅞ × 44-inch strip

- ✦ Cut four more 2½ × 44-inch strips. From these strips, cut thirty-six 2½ × 4½-inch rectangles.

Plan Ahead

When you cut out the pieces for the blocks in Pine Valley, plan to cut out three extra blocks, and set them aside to make a vertical wall quilt or table runner that coordinates with your quilt. You can use the same size side and corner triangles, and border widths, too.

From the wheat print fabric:
- ✦ Cut eighteen 2½ × 44-inch strips. From these strips, cut seventy-two 2½ × 10½-inch rectangles.

- ✦ Cut two more 2½ × 44-inch strips. From these strips, cut eighteen 2½-inch squares.

- ✦ Cut one 2⅞ × 44-inch strip

From the gold print fabric:
- ✦ Cut two 2½ × 44-inch strips. From these strips, cut eighteen 2½-inch squares.

From the brown check fabric:
- ✦ Cut three 2½ × 44-inch strips. From these strips, cut thirty-six 2½-inch squares.

Piecing

1 Layer the 2⅞ × 44-inch brown and wheat strips together, press, and cut them into nine 2⅞-inch squares, taking care not to shift the layers as you work. Cut the layered squares in half diagonally. Stitch ¼ inch away from the diagonal edges, as shown in **Diagram 1,** and press. At this point, the 18 triangle-pieced squares should measure 2½ inches square.

Diagram 1

2 Sew a triangle-pieced square and a 2½ × 6½-inch green rectangle together, as shown in **Diagram 2,** and press. Make a total of 18 of these units.

Diagram 2

3 Position a 2½-inch wheat square on the corner of a 2½ × 4½-inch brown rectangle, as shown at top left in **Diagram 3.** Stitch diagonally on the wheat square, trim the seam allowance to ¼ inch, and press, as shown at top right. Make a total of 18 of these units, and sew them to the remaining 2½ × 6½-inch green rectangles, as shown at the bottom of the diagram.

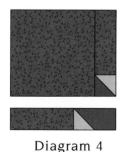

Diagram 3

4 Sew the Step 2 units to the right edge of the 8½-inch green squares, as shown in **Diagram 4,** and press. Sew the Step 3 units to the bottom edge of the green squares, as shown, and press, making the tree units.

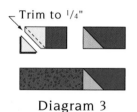

Diagram 4

5 Position a 2½-inch brown print square on the corner of a 2½ × 10½-inch wheat rectangle, as shown in **Diagram 5.** Stitch diagonally on the brown square, as shown, and trim the seam allowance to ¼ inch. Press the seam allowance toward the lighter fabric to eliminate bulky seams and to help the pieces nestle together more easily. Make a total of 18 of these units, as shown at the bottom of the diagram.

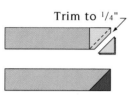

Diagram 5

6 Sew a 2½ × 10½-inch wheat rectangle to the left edge of each tree unit, as shown in **Diagram 6.** Sew the Step 5 units to the right edge of each tree unit, as shown, and press.

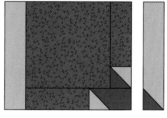

Diagram 6

7 Sew a 2½-inch gold square to the left edge of a 2½ × 10½-inch wheat rectangle, as shown in **Diagram 7.** Sew a 2½-inch brown check square to the right edge of the wheat rectangle, as shown, and press. Make a total of 18 of these units.

Diagram 7

8 Position a 2½ × 4½-inch brown rectangle on the right corner of a 2½ × 10½-inch wheat rectangle, as shown at the top of **Diagram 8.** Stitch diagonally on the brown rectangle, as shown, and trim the seam allowance to ¼ inch. Press the seam allowance toward the lighter fabric to eliminate bulky seams and to help the pieces nestle together more easily. Sew a 2½-inch brown check square to the left edge of the wheat rectangle, and press. Make a total of 18 of these units, as shown at the bottom of the diagram.

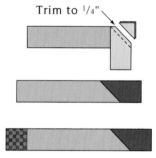

Diagram 8

9 Sew the Step 7 units to the top of the tree units, as shown in **Diagram 9.** Sew the Step 8 units to the bottom of the tree units, as shown, and press. Make a total of 18 Tree Blocks. At this point, the Tree Blocks should measure 14½ inches square.

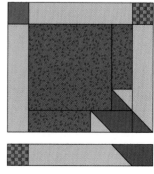

Diagram 9

Quilt Center

The side and corner triangles are larger than necessary and will be trimmed after they have been added to the Tree Blocks.

Cutting

From the red print fabric:

✦ Cut three 22-inch squares. Cut these into quarters diagonally to make 12 side triangles. You will be using 10 side triangles.

✦ Cut two 14-inch squares. Cut these in half diagonally to make four corner triangles.

Assembly

When sewing the blocks into diagonal rows, press the seam allowances between blocks in the opposite direction from those in the previous row. This will allow for easy matching and sewing at the block intersections.

1 Sew the Tree Blocks together in diagonal rows, as shown in **Diagram 10,** beginning and ending each row with side triangles as needed. Do not attach the corner triangles yet.

2 Referring to **Diagram 10,** sew the diagonal rows together, pinning the block intersections for accuracy. Press all seam allowances between rows in the same direction.

3 Sew the corner triangles to the quilt top, referring to **Diagram 10.**

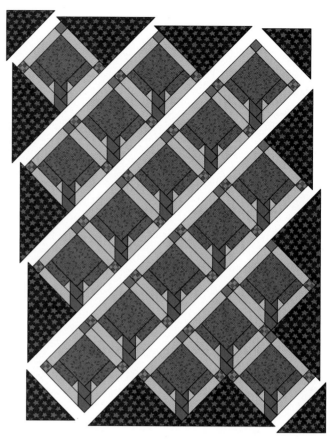

Diagram 10

4 Trim the excess fabric from the side and corner triangles, taking care to include the ¼-inch seam allowance needed at the corners of each block beyond the block corners of the quilt. Before beginning to trim, take time to read "Trimming Side and Corner Triangles" on page 196 to be assured of making these cuts accurately.

Borders

The yardage given allows for the inner and outer border strips to be cut on the crosswise grain. The border strips are longer than necessary and will be trimmed later.

Cutting

From the dark green print fabric:

✦ Cut eight 2½ × 44-inch strips for the inner border

From the brown check fabric:

✦ Cut nine 6½ × 44-inch strips for the outer border

Attaching the Borders

1 To attach the 2½-inch-wide dark green inner border strips, as shown in the **Quilt Diagram** on page 177, refer to page 198 for "Border Instructions."

2 To attach the 6½-inch-wide brown check outer border strips, as shown in the **Quilt Diagram,** refer to page 198 for "Border Instructions."

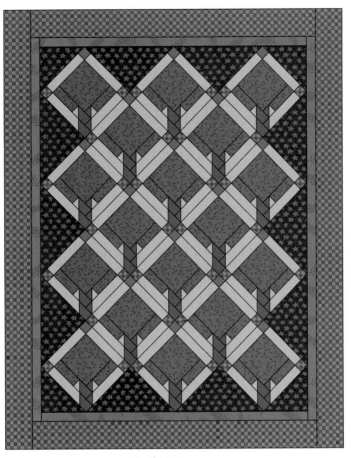

Quilt Diagram

PUTTING IT ALL TOGETHER

1 Cut the 5½-yard length of backing fabric in half crosswise to make two 2¾-yard lengths. Remove the selvages and sew the long edges together. Press the seam allowances open. Trim the backing and batting so they are about 4 inches larger than the quilt top.

2 For quilting ideas, see the **Quilting Design Diagram.** See page 201 for detailed marking, layering, and finishing instructions.

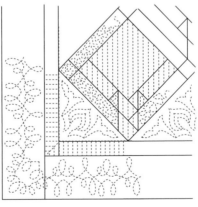

Quilting Design Diagram

BINDING

The 2¾-inch binding strips will produce a ½-inch-wide finished binding. If you want a wider or narrower binding, adjust the width of the strips you cut. (See page 201 for pointers on how to experiment with binding width.) Refer to "Attaching Binding with Mitered Corners" on page 202 to complete your quilt.

Cutting Crosswise Strips

From the brown print binding fabric:

◆ Cut nine 2¾ × 44-inch strips on the crosswise grain

HOUSE DRESSING

Double-Ruffled Pillow Sham

Finished Pillow Sham: 20 × 28 inches
(without ruffle)

FABRICS AND SUPPLIES

+ 1 yard green print #1 fabric for pillow top and back

+ 1⅓ yards green print #2 fabric for mock outer ruffle and ties

+ ½ yard red print fabric for mock inner ruffle

+ ¼ yard gold print fabric for binding

+ 20 × 26-inch bed pillow

+ Rotary cutter, mat, and wide see-through ruler with ⅛-inch markings

Cutting

From the green print #1 fabric:
+ Cut two 21 × 28-inch rectangles for the pillow top and back

From the green print #2 fabric:
+ Cut four 5 × 44-inch strips. Cut each strip in half crosswise for eight ties.

+ Cut four 5½ × 44-inch strips for the outer ruffle

From the red print fabric:
+ Cut four 3½ × 44-inch strips for the inner ruffle

From the gold print fabric:
+ Cut two 3 × 44-inch strips for the binding

Ties

1 Fold the eight 5 × 22-inch green print #2 strips in half lengthwise. With right sides together, stitch the long raw edges together, with a diagonal seam at one end, as shown in **Diagram 1.** Trim the seam allowances to ¼ inch at the ends. Leave the other end of each tie unstitched. Turn the ties right side out, and press. Make a total of eight ties.

Trim to ¼"—

Diagram 1

2 With raw edges even, position the ties on the wrong side of each 21 × 28-inch pillow section, as shown in **Diagram 2,** placing them 6 inches in from the long edges of the pillow, as shown. Baste the ties in place, and pin the other ends to the pillow sections, to keep them out of the way while adding the ruffle. Add ties to the opposite ends of each pillow section in the same manner.

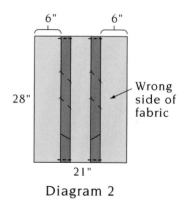

6"   6"

28"

Wrong side of fabric

21"

Diagram 2

3 With the right sides of the pillow sections together, sew one side seam, and open up the pillow sham, as shown in **Diagram 3.**

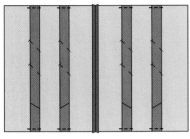

Diagram 3

Ruffle

1 To make the ruffle for one end of the pillow sham, diagonally piece two 3½ × 44-inch red strips together and two 5½ × 44-inch green strips together, referring to page 198 for "Diagonal Piecing."

2 With right sides together, sew the red and green strips together along one long edge. Fold the strip in half lengthwise, wrong sides together, and press. With raw edges even, run a gathering stitch ¼ inch from the raw edges, as shown in **Diagram 4.**

Press fold

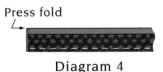

Diagram 4

3 With raw edges even and wrong sides together, position the ruffle over the ties, as shown in **Diagram 5.** Distribute the ruffle fullness evenly, while pulling up the gathering stitching, and sew the ruffle in place.

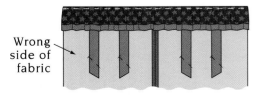

Wrong side of fabric

Diagram 5

4 Repeat Steps 1, 2, and 3 to make another ruffle, and sew it to the other end of the pillow sham in the same manner.

Double-Fold Binding

1 Fold the two 3 × 44-inch gold strips in half lengthwise, with wrong sides together, and press.

2 With raw edges even, lay the binding over the ruffle, as shown in **Diagram 6.** Stitch through the binding, ruffle, ties, and the pillow fabric ⅜ inch from raw edges. Remove the pins from the ties.

Ruffle, binding, ties, & pillow raw edges

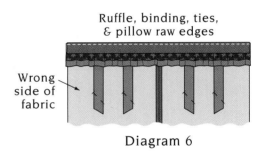

Wrong side of fabric

Diagram 6

3 Repeat Steps 1 and 2 at the other end of the pillow sham.

Finishing

1 At each end of the pillow sham, smooth the ruffle out flat and press the binding over the raw edges. Pin binding to pillow sham, being careful to keep the ties free. Topstitch the folded edge of the binding to the pillow sham.

2 Sew the remaining side seam, including the ruffles, and turn the pillow sham right side out. Insert a bed pillow, and tie the ties at each end of the pillow sham, referring to the photograph on page 173.

SNOW GOOSE

SIZE

Lap Quilt: 62 × 76 inches (unquilted)
Finished Block: 10 inches square

HOUSE DRESSING

See the Coordinating Comforter underneath the quilt on the bed.
Directions are given on page 184.

FABRICS AND SUPPLIES

Yardage is based on 44-inch-wide fabric.

✦ 3 yards blue print fabric for Plain Blocks, Flying Geese background, and inner border

✦ 1½ yards beige print fabric for Flying Geese

✦ 1⅞ yards large floral flannel print fabric for lattice posts and outer border

✦ ⅝ yard blue print fabric for binding

✦ 3¾ yards fabric for quilt backing

✦ Quilt batting, at least 66 × 80 inches

✦ Rotary cutter, mat, and wide see-through ruler with ⅛-inch markings

Getting Ready

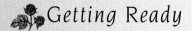

- Read instructions thoroughly before you begin.

- Prewash and press fabric.

- Place right sides of fabric pieces together and use ¼-inch seam allowances throughout unless directions specify otherwise.

- Seam allowances are included in the cutting sizes given.

- Press seam allowances in the direction that will create the least bulk, and whenever possible, press toward the darker fabric. Press border seam allowances toward the borders unless directions specify otherwise.

- Cutting directions for each section of the quilt are given individually. If you like to cut as you go, simply follow the directions as you get to them. If you'd rather cut all your pieces at the same time, skip ahead to find each of the cutting sections and do all the cutting before you begin.

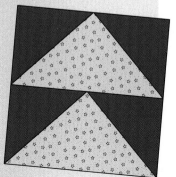

FABRIC KEY
(for the quilt shown on page 181)

■ Blue ▦ Beige ▨ Large floral

PLAIN BLOCKS
(Cut 12)

Cutting

From the blue print fabric:
+ Cut three 10½ × 44-inch strips. From these strips, cut twelve 10½-inch squares.

FLYING GEESE LATTICE STRIPS
(Make 31)

Cutting

From the beige print fabric:
+ Cut eighteen 2½ × 44-inch strips. From these strips, cut one hundred fifty-five 2½ × 4½-inch rectangles.

From the blue print fabric:
+ Cut nineteen 2½ × 44-inch strips. From these strips, cut three hundred ten 2½-inch squares.

Piecing

1 Position a 2½-inch blue square on the corner of a 2½ × 4½-inch beige rectangle, as shown at top left in **Diagram 1.** Stitch diagonally on the blue square, as shown. Trim the seam allowance to ¼ inch, and press, as shown at top right. Re-peat this process at the opposite corner of the beige rectangle, as shown at the bottom of the diagram. Make a total of 155 of these units.

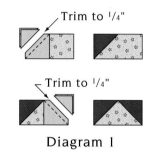

Diagram 1

2 Sew five units from Step 1 together to make a Flying Geese Lattice Strip, as shown in **Diagram 2,** and press. Make a total of 31 of these lattice strips. At this point, the lattice strips should measure 4½ × 10½ inches.

Diagram 2

QUILT CENTER

Cutting

From the large floral flannel print fabric:
+ Cut three 4½ × 44-inch strips. From these strips, cut twenty 4½-inch square lattice posts.

Piecing

1 Sew three Flying Geese Lattice Strips and four 4½-inch square floral lattice posts together, as shown in **Diagram 3**, and press. Make a total of five of these strips.

2 Sew four Flying Geese Lattice Strips and three 10½-inch square blue Plain Blocks together, as shown in **Diagram 4**, and press. Make a total of four of these strips.

3 Referring to the **Quilt Diagram** for the proper direction of the Flying Geese Lattice Strips, sew the five strips from Step 1 and the four strips from Step 2 together, and press.

Diagram 3

Diagram 4

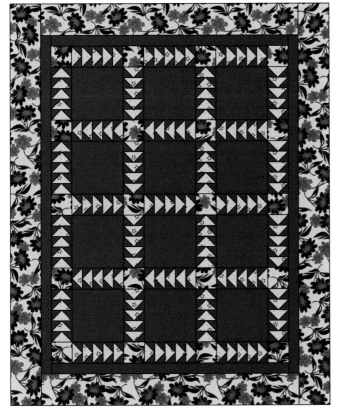

Quilt Diagram

As soon as you buy the flannel fabric for the lattice posts and outer border of Snow Goose, plan on washing it right away, so that it is preshrunk and ready to be used in your quilt. This is especially necessary in the case of flannel, which can shrink appreciably more than other cotton fabrics.

BORDERS

The yardage given allows for the border strips to be cut on the crosswise grain. The border strips are longer than necessary and will be trimmed later.

Cutting

From the blue print fabric:
✦ Cut seven 2½ × 44-inch strips for the inner border

From the large floral flannel print fabric:
✦ Cut seven 6½ × 44-inch strips for the outer border

Attaching the Borders

1 To attach the 2½-inch-wide blue inner border strips, as shown in the **Quilt Diagram,** refer to page 198 for "Border Instructions."

2 To attach the 6½-inch-wide floral outer border strips, refer to page 198 for "Border Instructions."

PUTTING IT ALL TOGETHER

1 Cut the 3¾-yard length of backing fabric in half crosswise to make two 1⅞-yard lengths. Remove the selvages and sew the long edges together. Press the seam allowance open. Trim the backing and batting so they are about 4 inches larger than the quilt top.

2 For quilting ideas, see the **Quilting Design Diagram.** See page 201 for detailed marking, layering, and finishing instructions.

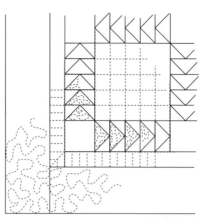

Quilting Design Diagram

BINDING

The 2¾-inch binding strips will produce a ½-inch-wide finished binding. If you want a wider or narrower binding, adjust the width of the strips you cut. (See page 201 for pointers on how to experiment with binding width.) Refer to "Attaching Binding with Mitered Corners" on page 202 to complete your quilt.

Cutting Crosswise Strips

From the blue print binding fabric:
✦ Cut seven 2¾ × 44-inch strips on the crosswise grain

HOUSE DRESSING

Coordinating Comforter

Finished Comforter: 81 × 96 inches

FABRICS AND SUPPLIES

✦ 81 × 96-inch quilt batting

✦ Two 81 × 96-inch pieces of contrasting flannel fabric

✦ 1⅞ yards fabric for binding

1 Layer and baste the flannel fabrics with right sides facing out and the batting sandwiched between them, and quilt as desired.

2 Cut ten 6½ × 44-inch strips of binding fabric for 1-inch-wide, finished double-fold binding. Piece the binding strips together with diagonal seams, trim the seam allowances to ¼ inch, and press the seams open.

3 Sew the binding to the right side of the comforter with a 1-inch seam allowance, mitering the corners. For more information on binding, see "Attaching Binding with Mitered Corners" on page 202. Fold the binding to the back side of the comforter and hand stitch it in place.

Joanne Wilson
General Engineering Professor

My Life When I'm Not Quilting

Teaching four general engineering classes at the University of Wisconsin—Platteville each semester keeps me actively involved in campus life. I love the challenge and intellectual stimulation that come from choosing a career in higher education.

Why I Quilt

There's something about playing with fabric and seeing it come to life in a quilt that I find exciting. It's wonderful to be able to sit down and start sewing on a Friday night or Saturday morning and have something beautiful to show for it by Sunday.

My Most Memorable Project

One year for Christmas, I made a lap-size quilt for each of my four nephews and two nieces. On Christmas night, we held an impromptu photo session and took pictures of each child holding his or her quilt, and a group photo of all of us together—everyone loved the quilts because they'd been made especially for them.

My Best Tip for Finding More Time for Quilting

Cut out the fabric for more than one quilt at the same time. That way, after you finish one project, you'll have everything for your next project all precut and ready to start working on. And if you can leave your sewing machine out at all times, you'll save time by not having to set it up every time you want to quilt.

The quilts you make and love to have around you project your feelings or moods in a way that nothing else can.

—Joanne Wilson

CONNECTING BLOCKS

SIZE

Bed Quilt: 76 × 94 inches (unquilted)
Finished Block: 12 inches square

FABRICS AND SUPPLIES

Yardage is based on 44-inch-wide fabric.

+ ⅔ yard beige print fabric for Pieced Blocks

+ 1¾ yards gold print fabric for Pieced Blocks,
  Nine Patch Blocks, and Connector Blocks

+ ⅔ yard chestnut print fabric for Pieced Blocks

+ 2¼ yards small green floral fabric for Connector Blocks

+ 1¼ yards red print #1 fabric for Pieced Blocks and
  inner border

+ ¾ yard red print #2 fabric for Nine Patch Blocks

+ 2⅜ yards large green floral fabric for Pieced Blocks and
  outer border

+ ⅞ yard red print #1 fabric for binding

+ 5½ yards fabric for quilt backing

+ Quilt batting, at least 80 × 98 inches

+ Rotary cutter, mat, and wide see-through ruler
  with ⅛-inch markings

Color Play

See page 188 for a creative color variation
on the quilt shown here.

Getting Ready

- Read instructions thoroughly before you begin.

- Prewash and press fabric.

- Place right sides of fabric pieces together and use ¼-inch seam allowances throughout unless directions specify otherwise.

- Seam allowances are included in the cutting sizes given.

- Press seam allowances in the direction that will create the least bulk, and whenever possible, press toward the darker fabric. Press border seam allowances toward the borders unless directions specify otherwise.

- Cutting directions for each section of the quilt are given individually. If you like to cut as you go, simply follow the directions as you get to them. If you'd rather cut all your pieces at the same time, skip ahead to find each of the cutting sections and do all the cutting before you begin.

☐ Beige	☐ Gold	☐ Chestnut
Small green floral	Red #1	Red #2 · Large green floral

Color Play

The beige Connector Blocks in this color variation quilt feature a small floral print, just as in the same blocks in the quilt on page 187. Here, the lighter shade of beige makes them act like a background, while the darker Pieced Blocks and Nine Patch Blocks are visually more prominent.

PIECED BLOCKS

(Make 12)

Cutting

From the gold print fabric:
✦ Cut six 2½ × 44-inch strips

From the beige print fabric:
✦ Cut six 2½ × 44-inch strips

**From the large
green floral fabric:**
✦ Cut twelve 4½-inch squares

From the red print #1 fabric:
✦ Cut six 2½ × 44-inch strips

**From the chestnut
print fabric:**
✦ Cut six 2½ × 44-inch strips

Piecing

1 To make the four patch units, sew the gold and beige 2½-inch-wide strips together in pairs, as shown in **Diagram 1,** and press. Make six of Strip Set I, as shown, and cross cut them into ninety-six 2½-inch segments.

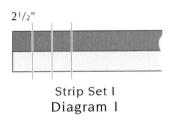

2½"

Strip Set I
Diagram 1

2 Sew the Step 1 segments together in pairs, as shown in **Diagram 2,** to make 48 four patch units.

Diagram 2

3 Sew the red and chestnut 2½-inch-wide strips together in pairs, as shown in **Diagram 3,** and press. Make six of Strip Set II, as shown, and cross cut them into forty-eight 4½-inch segments.

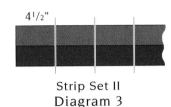

4½"

Strip Set II
Diagram 3

4 Sew a Step 3 segment to the top and bottom of each 4½-inch green floral square, placing the red fabric next to the green floral square, as shown in **Diagram 4,** and press.

Diagram 4

5 Sew a four patch unit to opposite sides of the remaining Step 3 units, as shown in **Diagram 5,** and press. Sew these units to both sides of the Step 4 units, as shown, and press. Make a total of 12 Pieced Blocks. At this point, the Pieced Blocks should measure 12½ inches square.

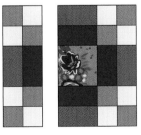

Diagram 5

NINE PATCH BLOCKS

(Make 20)

Cutting

From the gold print fabric:
✦ Cut eight 2½ × 44-inch strips

From the red print #2 fabric:
✦ Cut seven 2½ × 44-inch strips

Piecing

1 Sew a gold strip to each side of three of the red strips to make Strip Set I, as shown in **Diagram 6,** and press. Cross cut the strip sets into forty 2½-inch segments.

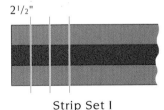

2½"

Strip Set I
Diagram 6

2 Sew a red strip to each side of the two remaining gold strips to make Strip Set II, as shown in **Diagram 7,** and press. Cross cut the strip sets into twenty 2½-inch segments.

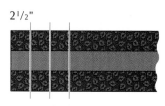

2½"

Strip Set II
Diagram 7

3 Sew a Step 1 unit to each side of the Step 2 units, as shown in **Diagram 8.** Make a total of 20 Nine Patch blocks. At this point, the Nine Patch Blocks should measure 6½ inches square.

Diagram 8

CONNECTOR BLOCKS

(Make 31)

Cutting

From the small green floral fabric:
✦ Cut eleven 6½ × 44-inch strips. From these strips, cut thirty-one 6½ × 12½-inch rectangles.

From the gold print fabric:
✦ Cut eight 2½ × 44-inch strips. From these strips, cut one hundred twenty-four 2½-inch squares.

Piecing

Position a 2½-inch gold square on each of the four corners of the 6½ × 12½-inch green floral rectangles, as shown at the top of **Diagram 9.** Stitch diagonally on the gold squares, trim the seam allowances to ¼ inch, and press, as shown at the bottom of the diagram. Make a total of 31 Connector Blocks. At this point, the Connector Blocks should measure 6½ × 12½ inches.

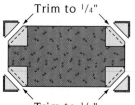

Trim to ¼"

Trim to ¼"

Diagram 9

QUILT CENTER

Assembly

1 Sew three Pieced Blocks and four Connector Blocks together, as shown in **Diagram 10,** and press. Make a total of four of these rows.

2 Sew three Connector Blocks and four Nine Patch Blocks together, as shown in **Diagram 11,** and press. Make a total of five of these rows.

3 Referring to the **Quilt Diagram** on page 191, sew the rows together to form the quilt center, and press.

BORDERS

The yardage given allows for the border strips to be cut on the crosswise grain. The border strips are longer than necessary and will be trimmed later.

Cutting

From the red print #1 fabric:
✦ Cut eight 2½ × 44-inch strips for the inner border

Diagram 10

Diagram 11

Quilt Diagram

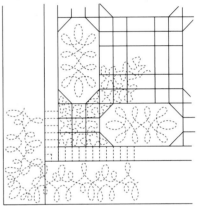

Quilting Design Diagram

From the large green floral fabric:

- ✦ Cut nine 6½ × 44-inch strips for the outer border

Attaching the Borders

1 To attach the 2½-inch-wide red inner border strips, as shown in the **Quilt Diagram,** refer to page 198 for "Border Instructions."

2 To attach the 6½-inch-wide green floral outer border strips, refer to page 198 for "Border Instructions."

PUTTING IT ALL TOGETHER

1 Cut the 5½-yard length of backing fabric in half crosswise to make two 2¾-yard lengths. Remove the selvages and sew the long edges together. Press the seam allowance open. Trim the backing and batting so they are about 4 inches larger than the quilt top.

2 For quilting ideas, see the **Quilting Design Diagram.** See page 201 for detailed marking, layering, and finishing instructions.

BINDING

The 2¾-inch binding strips will produce a ½-inch-wide finished binding. If you want a wider or narrower binding, adjust the width of the strips you cut. (See page 201 for pointers on how to experiment with binding width.) Refer to "Attaching Binding with Mitered Corners" on page 202 to complete your quilt.

Cutting Crosswise Strips

From the red print #1 binding fabric:

- ✦ Cut nine 2¾ × 44-inch strips on the crosswise grain

RESOURCES FOR BUSY QUILTERS

Busy quilters everywhere know that using efficient and successful techniques and having the supplies you need at your fingertips, right when you need them, are among the best ways to make the most of your time. In the first part of this "Resources for Busy Quilters" section, you'll find innovative techniques for making quilts easily and quickly. Following that section are useful lists of mail-order suppliers and Internet Web sites that will help you locate the perfect supplies for your every quilt-making need. The most up-to-the-minute quiltmaking tools and supplies are just a phone call or click away.

Main Street Cotton Shop
7 North Main St.
Hutchinson, Mn. 55350
(320) 234-7298

Thimbleberries, Inc.
7 North Main St.
Hutchinson, Mn.
55350
(320) 587-3944

TIMESAVING TECHNIQUES

Easy, streamlined, and quick techniques form the basis for all of the quilts and companion projects I've designed for this book. You can have confidence that your results will be great every time. I've also included several of my own special tips and tricks for effective ways to work with specialty fabrics like flannel and some simple ways to experiment with different binding widths.

FABRIC CHOICES

Use 100 percent cotton fabric or cotton flannel for making the projects in this book. Cotton is a perennial favorite with quilters because it is soft, lightweight, and easy to stitch and press. And the wide array of cotton flannels now available makes this fabric another great choice for soft, casual quilts. These simple guidelines will help you get great results with flannel every time.

Fabulous Flannels

◆ Always prewash and machine dry flannel fabric to prevent severe shrinkage in a finished quilt. Because some flannels can shrink more than others, we have taken care to allow approximately ¼ yard extra for each flannel listed under the Fabrics and Supplies lists in this book.

◆ Because flannel is stretchier than other cotton fabrics and it has a nap that makes it thicker, the quilt design you choose should be simple, to allow the color and texture of flannel fabrics to make their own design statement.

◆ Treat the more heavily napped side of a *solid* color flannel fabric as the right side of the fabric.

◆ Consider combining regular cotton calicos with flannels. The different textures complement each other nicely.

◆ Lengthen the stitch length setting on your sewing machine to 10 to 12 stitches per inch to avoid stretching or puckering, and use a standard ¼-inch seam allowance.

◆ Press flannel gently, to avoid stretching pieces out of shape.

◆ Because flannel tends to shift during the stitching process, it is possible to end up with misshapen blocks. As you stitch the pieces of a block together, take time to stop and check measurements as you go, and whenever necessary, square up the blocks.

◆ When sewing flannel triangle-pieced squares together, be especially careful not to stretch the diagonal seams, and trim away the points from the seam allowances to eliminate bulk.

- If one piece of flannel seems to stretch more than another piece, position the stretchier one on the bottom as it goes through the sewing machine. The natural action of the feed dogs will help minimize or prevent stretching.

- Another trick for minimizing distortions is to place straight pins at close intervals when joining two pieces of flannel. If you are working with very long pieces of flannel for borders, divide the pieces into quarters, pin them securely with straight pins, and continue dividing the sections into smaller sections and pin them together closely.

- Use a lightweight batting with flannel, to prevent your quilt from becoming too heavy.

- Quilt in the ditch or straight stitch as much as possible, to eliminate the need for marking, which can be difficult because of the nap of flannel fabric.

- To highlight hand-quilting stitches on flannel, use size #8 or #12 pearl cotton and a slightly longer stitch length than you would choose for other cotton fabrics.

TOOLS AND EQUIPMENT

Making beautiful quilts does not require a large number of specialized tools or expensive equipment. My list of favorites is short and sweet, and includes the things I use over and over again because they are always accurate and dependable.

- I find a long acrylic ruler indispensable for accurate rotary cutting. The ones I like most are an Omnigrid 6 × 24-inch grid acrylic ruler for cutting long strips and squaring up fabrics and quilt tops, and a "Masterpiece 45" 8 × 24-inch ruler for cutting 6- to 8-inch-wide borders. I sometimes tape together two 6 × 24-inch acrylic rulers for cutting borders up to 12 inches wide (see Bachelor Quarters, page 76).

- A 15-inch Omnigrid square acrylic ruler is great for squaring up individual blocks and corners of a quilt top, for cutting strips up to 15 inches wide or long, and for trimming side and corner triangles.

- I think the markings on my 23 × 35-inch Olfa rotary cutting mat stay visible longer than on other mats, and the lines are fine and accurate.

- The largest size Olfa rotary cutter cuts through many layers of fabric easily, and it isn't cumbersome to use. The 2½-inch blade slices through three layers of backing, batting, and a quilt top like butter.

- An 8-inch pair of Gingher shears is great for cutting out appliqué templates and cutting fabric from a bolt or fabric scraps.

- I keep a pair of 5¼-inch Gingher scissors by my sewing machine, so it's handy for both machine work and handwork. This size is versatile and sharp enough to make large and small cuts equally well.

- My Grabbit magnetic pin cushion has a surface that's large enough to hold lots of straight pins, and a strong magnet that keeps them securely in place.

- Silk pins are long and thin, which means they won't leave large holes in your fabric. I like them because they increase accuracy in pinning pieces or blocks together, and it's easy to press over silk pins, as well.

- For pressing individual pieces, blocks, and quilt tops, I use an 18 × 48-inch sheet of plywood covered with several layers of cotton fiberfill and topped with a layer of muslin stapled to the

back. The 48-inch length allows me to press an entire width of fabric at one time without the need to reposition it, and the square ends are better than tapered ends on an ironing board for pressing finished quilt tops.

ROTARY CUTTING

For best results in rotary cutting the pieces for a quilt, start by folding your fabric so that it lies wrinkle-free on your cutting table, and use these tips to ensure accuracy.

Starting Out Straight

Before you begin to cut, square off the left end of your fabric by lining up the selvages and placing an acrylic square ruler along the fold, as shown in **Diagram 1**. Position a 6 × 24-inch acrylic ruler against the side of the square in order to determine a true 90-degree angle from the folded edge. Holding the ruler firmly in place, remove the square, and cut along the long edge of the ruler.

NOTE: *If you are left-handed, work from the other end of the fabric.*

6" × 24" ruler

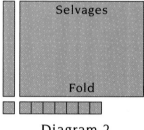

Diagram 1

Cutting Strips, Squares, and Rectangles

Cut strips on the cross-wise grain of the fabric, as shown in **Diagram 2**, unless the instructions indicate otherwise. Cut the strips into squares or rectangles, as indicated for each project.

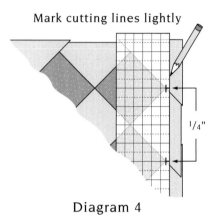

Diagram 2

Make it a habit to stop often and make sure that the left edge of the fabric stays at a 90-degree angle to the folded edge of your fabric. This will help keep your strips straight, rather than angled, as shown in **Diagram 3**. If necessary, refold the fabric, square up the left edge again, and continue cutting.

Diagram 3

Trimming Side and Corner Triangles

To trim oversize side and corner triangles before adding the borders to a quilt, use a rotary cutter, cutting mat, and wide acrylic ruler, and follow these steps.

1 Beginning at one corner of your quilt, line up the acrylic ruler ¼ inch beyond the points of the corners of the blocks, as shown in **Diagram 4**. Lightly mark the cutting line along the edge of the ruler, as shown. Repeat this step on all four sides of the quilt top.

Mark cutting lines lightly

1/4"

Diagram 4

2 Before you begin to do any cutting, check the markings at all four corners of your quilt top to make absolutely sure the lines are at 90-degree angles to each other, as shown in **Diagram 5**. Now is the time to adjust your marked cutting lines, if necessary, to ensure square corners on your quilt top. When you are certain that everything is straight and true, align the acrylic ruler with your marked lines, and cut away the excess fabric of the side and corner triangles. This will leave an accurate ¼-inch seam allowance on all four sides and beyond the block corners.

Make sure corners are 90° angles before you cut

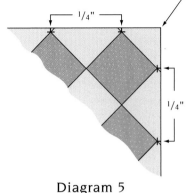

Diagram 5

DECORATIVE STITCHES

Many of my quilt designs feature fusible appliqué, which is quick and easy to do, following the instructions given in each project. My favorite decorative stitches for enhancing appliqué motifs are the buttonhole stitch, shown at the top of **Diagram 6,** and the stem stitch, shown at the bottom of the diagram. Buttonhole stitching is a good choice for outlining appliquéd shapes,

and the stem stitch is nice for adding details, like veins on leaves or gores on a pumpkin.

Give some of these tips a try on projects like My Favorite Things on page 30, Slice of Summer Table Runner on page 40, Flurries on page 132, or A Patch of Pumpkins on page 156.

✦ I like to use black or a contrasting thread color for making something appear visually prominent in a quilt, like the center of a flower or veins in a leaf. You can also replicate the look of a vintage 1930s quilt by outlining light-colored or pastel appliqué shapes in black, as in the Appliquéd Tablecloth on page 169.

✦ One strand of #8 pearl cotton or three strands of embroidery floss will be thick enough to add texture and dimension to an appliqué motif, while remaining easy to pull through the fabric. I prefer pearl cotton because it does not need

to be split into separate strands, and it has a lovely sheen.

✦ A package of assorted embroidery sharps contains a wide range of needle sizes, which are great for experimenting with different types of threads. For buttonhole stitching, the eye of your needle should be large enough to make threading easy. I avoid crewel needles, even though they do have long eyes, because they aren't as sharp as embroidery needles.

✦ Experiment with a variety of interesting, heavier-weight threads for buttonhole stitching—see what you think of hand-dyed pearl cottons, wool crewel yarns, or shiny metallic fibers. Whenever I need a specific or unusual thread color, I turn to embroidery floss because it's widely stocked and available in hundreds of shades.

MACHINE APPLIQUÉ

Although most of the quilts in the photographs in this book feature fusible appliqué, my quilt designs are also lovely when appliquéd by machine. If you like the look of satin-stitched motifs, explore the possibilities of some of these helpful hints.

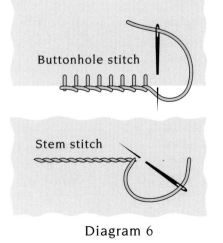

Buttonhole stitch

Stem stitch

Diagram 6

✦ I like stabilizing the background fabric for machine appliqué by placing a paper towel underneath it while satin stitching. The paper towel adds weight to the fabric, which helps support the large amount of thread accumulating in a very small area of the fabric. The paper pulls away very easily after the appliqué is finished—plus it's inexpensive and available at any grocery store.

✦ Use the medium width zigzag stitch on *your* sewing machine to get the best results in your machine appliqué. I do not like to specify a particular stitch width because all sewing machines are different. My guideline is that if your satin stitching is too narrow, it will not hold an appliqué piece securely in place, while satin stitching that's too wide can look heavy and make it difficult to turn corners and stitch smoothly around curves. One place where a narrow satin stitch width is perfect is for putting in details, such as stem veins.

✦ Try using two threads through the needle on top of your machine, and a single thread in the bobbin for machine appliqué or decorative stitching. Treating the two top threads as one will create a heavier, raised, almost embossed

look in either satin stitching or buttonhole stitching. Experiment till you find the stitch width on your machine that pleases you.

✦ I like to match the color of my top thread or threads to the fabric in each appliqué when I satin stitch because it makes the stitched shapes look embellished and highlighted, rather than outlined.

BORDER INSTRUCTIONS

Beautiful borders are the perfect finishing touch to a quilt. The instructions in this book call for cutting border strips that are longer than necessary and trimming them to the correct size later. Here are some helpful hints for piecing and attaching borders so they lie smooth and flat, with perfectly square corners.

Diagonal Piecing

✦ For borders that are longer than 42 inches, piece the border strips together with diagonal seams, which are less visible in a finished quilt than straight seams. Diagonal seams work better for quilting, too, because they eliminate the possibility of a seam recurring in the same spot in a quilting design

throughout a quilt. The exception to this rule is when matching plaids or other printed or directional fabrics that look better with straight seams.

✦ To sew two border strips together diagonally, place them together at a 90-degree angle with right sides together, as shown in **Diagram 7.** Each strip should extend ¼ inch beyond the other. Sew the two strips together, taking care to start and stop your stitching precisely at the V-shaped notches where the two strips meet, as shown. Trim away the excess fabric, leaving a ¼-inch seam allowance, and press the seam open.

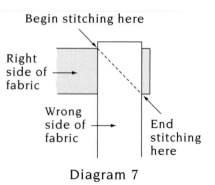

Diagram 7

✦ Cut enough border strips so that after your strips are stitched together, the diagonal seams will not fall at the corners of the quilt top.

Plaid Borders

I like to give guidelines, rather than steadfast rules, for working with plaid borders because many quilters like the casual look that comes from cutting border strips without planning the placement of the plaid. If you like the look of carefully planned plaid borders, try these tips and techniques.

✦ When cutting woven plaids on cross grain, cut along a single thread. This will ensure that the plaid stays perpendicular. (When cutting cross-grain borders from other types of fabrics, this is not necessary.) If your plaid border strips need to be longer than the 45-inch fabric width, cut them on the lengthwise grain to avoid piecing entirely. I think it is worth any extra expense to have a plaid border that is uninterrupted by any seams.

✦ Cut all four border strips so they will contain the same pattern repeat. This usually means you will need to use scissors, rather than a rotary cutter, and cut along a single thread line in the plaid fabric. Depending on the plaid you've chosen, it may be necessary to leave a few inches between border strips unused, in order to make sure they fall on the same pattern repeat, as shown in **Diagram 8.**

✦ As you sew plaid border strips onto a quilt, take care to place the same portion of the plaid next

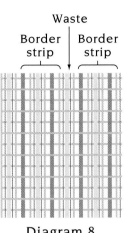

Waste

Border strip | Border strip

Diagram 8

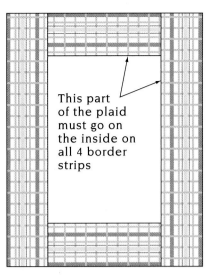

This part of the plaid must go on the inside on all 4 border strips

Diagram 9

to the quilt on each side. The more complicated the plaid, the more there will be to consider, as shown in **Diagram 9.**

✦ When I work with a plaid fabric that has printed motifs in it, I use a pair of scissors to cut the fabric on the cross grain, following a single thread line, and I make sure to place the borders so the motifs will point away from the center of the finished quilt top.

Attaching Borders

1 Mark the center points on all four sides of the quilt with straight pins, as shown in **Diagram 10.** To determine the length of the top and bottom border strips, measure the quilt from left to right through the middle. Mark the end points and the center point on each border strip with straight pins, as shown.

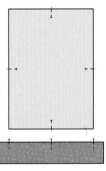

Diagram 10

2 Pin the top and bottom border strips to the quilt, matching end points and center points, as shown in **Diagram 11.** Stitch the top and bottom border strips to the quilt using a ¼-inch seam allowance. Press the seam allowances toward the borders, and trim away the excess border fabric.

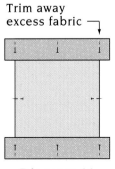

Trim away excess fabric

Diagram 11

3 To determine the length of the side border strips, measure the quilt from top to bottom through the middle, including the top and bottom borders.

4 Mark the end points and the center point on each side border strip with straight pins, as shown in **Diagram 12.** Stitch the side border strips to the quilt. Press and trim the side borders even with the top and bottom borders.

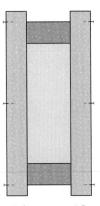

Diagram 12

5 If your quilt has multiple borders, measure, mark, and add the additional borders in the same manner.

Borders with Corner Squares

1 Sew the top and bottom border strips to the quilt, referring to Steps 1 and 2 under "Attaching Borders" on page 199. Press the borders, and trim away the excess border fabric in the same manner.

2 To determine the length of the side border strips,

measure the quilt top, including seam allowances, but *not* including the top and bottom borders. Cut the side border strips to this length.

3 Sew a corner square to each end of these border strips, sew the side borders to the quilt, as shown in **Diagram 13,** and press the seam allowances toward the borders.

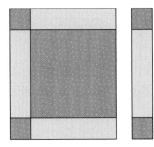

Diagram 13

4 If your quilt has multiple borders, measure, mark, and sew additional borders to the quilt in the same manner.

CHOOSING QUILTING DESIGNS

Quilting is an individual process that lets you create the look you like in your finished projects. My designs are appropriate for either hand or machine quilting. I'm always thinking of simple ways to quilt, so consider some of these ideas when it's time to choose hand or machine quilting designs for your next quilt.

◆ Repeating one of the pieced or appliquéd elements in a quilt as part of the quilting design will reemphasize that portion of the design.

◆ Two or three parallel rows of echo quilting outside an appliqué piece will highlight the shape effectively.

◆ Using #8 or #12 pearl cotton adds more visual weight to your quilting stitches and makes your quilting become part of the quilt's color scheme.

◆ Primitive stitch quilting with larger stitches adds a casual look to a quilt and takes away the pressure of hand quilting with very small stitches.

◆ Stipple quilting or meander quilting behind a feathered motif or a large, central motif will make the primary design appear to pop forward.

◆ Look for quilting designs that will cover two or more borders, rather than choosing separate designs for each individual border.

◆ Quilting in the ditch of seams is an effective way to get a project quilted without a lot of marking—a real time-saver!

◆ Try straight-line designs, like channel quilting, and space them at intervals that reflect a common width of a piece in the quilt. This will help to emphasize the design, while creating a feeling of continuity throughout the quilt.

Marking Quilting Designs

To mark a quilting design, use a commercially made stencil, make your own stencil, or trace designs from a printed source. If your marks will stay visible for a long time, mark the entire quilt top before layering. If you are using a powdered chalk marker or a chalk pencil, mark the quilting lines just before quilting them. The following markers are easy to see on fabric, and they will brush out or wear away easily after the quilting is finished. No matter what your choice, make sure to mark quilting designs very lightly for best results.

+ Quilter's silver pencil

+ Artist's white pencil

+ Chalk pencil or powdered chalk marker

+ Hard lead 0.5 millimeter pencil

+ Thin sliver of hand soap

LAYERING AND FINISHING

Follow these steps to prepare a quilt for quilting and finishing.

1 Cut your quilt backing 2 inches larger than your quilt top on all four sides. If it is necessary to piece the backing, cut off the selvages before sewing the lengths of fabric together.

2 Press the backing seam open, and place it so it will not lie at the center of your quilt. Try piecing different fabrics together to create an interesting quilt backing.

3 Open up your batting and allow it to relax overnight before layering the quilt. Then place the backing wrong side up on a flat surface. Lay the batting on top of the backing, and smooth it out evenly. Add the quilt top, right side up, and hand baste the three layers together with thread in a zigzag pattern, as shown in **Diagram 14.**

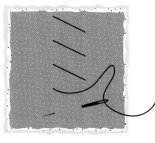

Diagram 14

4 After you've finished quilting, baste ¼ inch in from the cut edges on all four sides of your quilt to keep the layers from shifting and prevent puckers from forming when adding the binding. Trim the backing and batting even with the edges of your quilt top.

BINDING

The instructions indicate the width of the binding strips for each project in this book. If you use a high-loft batting or combine a fluffy batt with flannel fabrics, you may wish to vary the width of your binding strips, in order to encase the thicker edges of a quilt. Here's how.

Experimenting with Binding Width

+ For a thicker batting, add another ¼ to ½ inch to the cut width of your binding strips, and recalculate the binding yardage requirements.

+ Multiply the desired width of your binding by 6 to determine the width to cut your binding strips. For a ½-inch-wide finished binding, you will need to cut 3-inch-wide binding strips.

+ Start by increasing the cut width of your binding strips by ¼ inch, and do a test to see if that width will work. Cut a short length of binding, fold it in half, and lay it out on the edge of a quilt to make sure it will cover the edge and fold to the back side easily. Continue increasing the cut binding width by ¼ inch at a time until you discover what is best for your quilt.

Bias Binding and Diagonal Piecing

1 To cut bias binding strips, fold the binding yardage on the diagonal, forming a triangle, as shown in **Diagram 15.** Using a rotary cutter, mat, and wide acrylic ruler, measure in ½ inch from the fold, and cut away the folded edge. Move the ruler across the fabric, cutting parallel strips in the desired binding width.

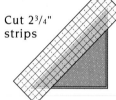

Cut 2¾" strips

Diagram 15

2 Diagonally piece the bias binding strips together, using as many longer strips as possible, with shorter strips placed between the longer ones. Place two strips together at a 90-degree angle, with right sides together, as shown at the top of **Diagram 16.** Each strip should extend ¼ inch beyond the other. Stitch across diagonally, making sure to start and end your stitching precisely at the V notches of

the two strips. Trim off the excess fabric, leaving a ¼-inch seam allowance, and press the seams open, as shown at the bottom of the diagram.

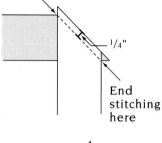

Begin stitching here

¼"

End stitching here

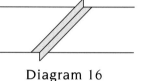

Diagram 16

Attaching Binding with Mitered Corners

1 After sewing the binding strips together, fold the binding in half lengthwise, wrong sides together, and press.

2 Unfold and cut the beginning end at a 45-degree angle, as shown in **Diagram 17.** Press the edge under ¼ inch, and refold the strip, as shown.

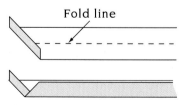

Fold line

Diagram 17

3 Begin attaching the binding along the bottom lower left side, rather than at a corner of your quilt.

4 With the raw edges of the binding and quilt top even, as shown in **Diagram 18,** start stitching about 2 inches from the diagonal cut end, using a ⅜-inch seam allowance. Stop stitching ⅜ inch from the corner, as shown in the diagram. Clip the thread and remove the quilt from the sewing machine.

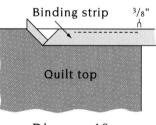

Binding strip ⅜"

Quilt top

Diagram 18

5 Fold the binding strip up and away from the corner of the quilt, forming a 45-degree angle, as shown in **Diagram 19.** Refold the binding down, so it is even with the raw edge of the quilt, as shown. Begin sewing at the upper edge, as shown. Miter all four corners in this manner.

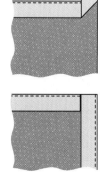

Diagram 19

6 As you approach the point where you started, trim the end of the binding, making sure the end is long enough to tuck inside the beginning of the binding, as shown in **Diagram 20,** and that the two ends overlap about ⅜ inch. Stitch the remaining binding to the quilt.

7 Turn the folded edge of the binding to the back side of the quilt, covering the stitching line, as shown in **Diagram 21.** Hand sew the binding in place, folding in the mitered corners as you go. Add several stitches to the folds of the miters on both the front and back to hold them in place, as shown.

Quilt back

Quilt back

Diagram 21

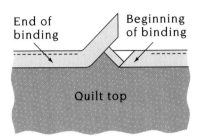

End of binding

Beginning of binding

Quilt top

Diagram 20

GETTING SUPPLIES THE FAST AND EASY WAY

Check with your local quilt shop first, for easy access and good service. If none is available, use this listing of mail-order fabric and tool sources with 800 numbers to get what you need fast. The Internet is quickly becoming a speedy source of quilting supplies, often at considerable discounts. If you have access to a computer, spend some time visiting the Web sites listed below. If you are leery of giving your credit card over the Internet, many sources offer alternative ways to place an order.

MAIL-ORDER SOURCES

Clotilde
Clotilde, Inc. B3000
Louisiana, MO 63353-3000
(800) 772-2891

Quilting and sewing books, patterns, notions, and supplies, including: Big Foot free-motion quilting foot, walking feet, fusible web, thimbles, markers, pins, needles, and rotary-cutting equipment

Keepsake Quilting
Route 25B, P.O. Box 1618
Centre Harbor, NH
03226-1618
(800) 865-9458

Quilting supplies and notions, including fabrics, patterns, quilt kits, the Little Foot presser foot, the Big Foot free-motion quilting foot, pins, needles, thimbles, templates, quilting frames and hoops, QuilTak basting tool, and battings

Lands' End
1 Lands' End Lane
Dodgeville, WI 53595
(800) 356-4444

The Original Attaché Case from Lands' End is great for holding quilting equipment, tools, markers, fabrics, paper, and more.

Main Street Cotton Shop
141 East 2nd Street
Redwood Falls, MN 56283
(800) 624-4001

A great source for quilting supplies, notions, fabrics, and kits—plus a mail-order catalog that features the entire line of Thimbleberries fabrics (both current as well as past)

Nancy's Notions
333 Beichl Avenue
P.O. Box 683
Beaver Dam, WI
53916-0683
(800) 833-0690

Sewing notions and supplies, including pins, needles, thimbles, presser feet, walking feet, fusible web, battings, and rotary-cutting equipment

Web of Thread

1410 Broadway
Paducah, KY 42001
(800) 955-8185

Quilting and sewing booklets, supplies, sewing machine needles, and a wide variety of machine quilting threads

INTERNET SOURCES

Clotilde, Inc.

http://www.clotilde.com/

Home base on the Internet for Clotilde, Inc. features the same books, notions, fabrics, patterns listed under Mail-Order Sources.

Cotton Club

http://www.cottonclub.com/index/html

Enrolling in a mail-order fabric club like "The Original Cottton Club" or "The Hoffman Club" will let you receive periodic mailings of 4-inch fabric samples of fabrics, like Hoffman batiks, metallics, and prints, plus a newsletter and information about great buys on books, notions, and tools.

Creative Quilting

http://www.thecreativeweb.com/quilting/quilting.html

Offers quilt books, batting, fabric, rotary cutting supplies and other quilting notions, quilt-related computer software, hoops, frames, portable sewing tables, and patterns.

The DMC Page

http://www.dmc-usa.com/

A complete listing of all threads manufactured by DMC, including pearl cotton; use the handy Store Search to locate the nearest source for DMC products in your area.

The Fabric Stash

http://fabric-stash.com/

Fabrics, books, patterns, kits, supplies, and gadgets—all available for order online or by phone. The handy Key Word Search helps you find exactly the notions and supplies you're looking for, and a helpful New Products listing lets you check out hot new products.

Hancock Fabrics

http://www2.hancocks-paducah.com/hancock/

Offers fabrics from Beatrix Potter, Benartex, Concord, Hoffman, Timeless Treasures, and more.

Lands' End

http://www.landsend.com

Visit this site to order the Lands' End Original Attaché Case and more.

Nancy's Notions

http://www.nancysnotions.com/

Nancy Zieman's online quilting and sewing store offers the same quilting and sewing products listed under Mail-Order Sources.

Quiltropolis

http://www.quiltropolis.com/

Batting, books, quilting notions, rotary cutting supplies, fabrics, quilt-related computer software, fabrics—including Thimbleberries Paint Box Colors

Quiltsearch

http://www.quiltsearch.com/Quilt/Index.html

Here's the perfect place to search out local quilt shops and find a wide array of quilting and sewing supplies. This Web site also has an extensive listing of other helpful textile and sewing-related links.

Tangled Threads

http://kbs-net/tt/

This site features quilt books, magazines, fabrics, notions, paper foundation patterns, and quilt-related computer software.

M·O·R·E A·B·O·U·T T·H·I·M·B·L·E·B·E·R·R·I·E·S

Throughout the year all of us here at Thimbleberries design studio are busy producing patterns for quilts and decorative home accessories that are sold around the world. My main goal is to design quilts and quilt accessories that will help you transform your home into a comfortable, inviting environment for you and your family. I want my designs to inspire you and also be easy, so you can make the projects no matter how busy your life is.

Thimbleberries has a complete line of individual patterns and books brimming with projects that can be quickly and easily accomplished. Our step-by-step, fully illustrated instructions will guide you through each project. These straightforward techniques will make each project a joy. To celebrate the holiday season, we offer a group of delightful Christmas books with all the trimmings— Santas and snowmen, soft sculptures, garlands, tree ornaments, wall quilts, table decorations, gifts, and packaging ideas. Color photographs and fully illustrated instructions will both inspire and guide you through these projects. To obtain a catalog, please write to Thimbleberries, Inc., 7 North Main Street, Hutchinson, MN 55350. To view our catalog online, visit our Web site at www.thimbleberries.com.

For the past five years I have been designing fabrics for RJR Fashion Fabrics. Each year approximately five lines of my fabrics are showcased at quality quilt shops around the world. These fabrics, in my signature palette of colors, along with the patterns and books, can help you achieve the Thimbleberries style. Look for Thimbleberries fabrics, patterns, and books at your local quilt shop.

P·H·O·T·O·G·R·A·P·H·Y C·R·E·D·I·T·S

All of the photography of the quilts in room settings took place in two specially designed sets in the Rodale Press Photography Studios in Emmaus, Pennsylvania. In the space of one week, these two sets were transformed into nine different rooms, with complete makeovers for the floors and walls. Wallpaper went up and came down and new coats of paint were applied following a tightly choreographed schedule. A liberal sprinkling of gold stars was stenciled from floor to ceiling in less time than it takes a cup of coffee to cool. A window even appeared, like magic, where a solid wall had been the day before. Entire roomfuls of furniture were whisked in and out several times a day. Props large and small flowed through the studio in a seemingly never-ending stream. These transformations happened thanks to the hard work and talents of the following people:

Carol Angstadt, Associate Art Director

One of the consummate organizers of all time, Carol made sure the master plan held together and everything happened when it needed to. On the shoot, Carol's artistic eye and sense of the book helped deliver photographs that showcased all the quilts at their best.

Nancy Smola Biltcliff, Designer

The mastermind of the original shoot schedule, Nancy plotted out which paint colors, flooring, furniture, and quilts needed to be on which set on any given day, at any given time. A pro at time management, Nancy even held off going into labor until the day she finalized the shoot schedule!

Lynette Jensen, Author

The style guide for this photographic adventure, Lynette flew to Pennsylvania carrying her own stencils and paint, plus suitcases full of personal props. Not afraid to roll up her sleeves, Lynette spent the week directing the shoot, arranging props, and making sure the quilts and their settings represented the Thimbleberries look she has created.

Marianne Laubach, Stylist

Always calm and unflappable, Marianne gathered dozens of pieces of furniture and hundreds of props and made sure everything showed up at the studios on time. On the sets, she helped capture the essence of the Thimbleberries style and was the "glue" that kept everything together and running smoothly.

Mitch Mandel, Photographer

Mitch's diligence behind the lens ensured that the charm of the quilts in their settings made its way onto film. This is the third book of Thimbleberries quilts that Mitch has photographed. When he stepped out from behind the camera, his woodworking talents emerged as he assembled beds and other pieces of furniture.

Fred Matlack, Set Design and Production

Fred made all the sets—a simple statement that belies the amazing effort and resourcefulness that he brought to the task. Every floorboard, coat of paint, and strip of wallpaper received his careful attention. His creative talents show in the decorative sponging and stenciling effects on the walls. No request made him flinch, not even when he realized he had to stencil stars over 96 square feet of walls in less than half an hour.

Glenn Milano, Photography Assistant

Adept at anticipating the need for a new lens or a film reload, Glenn also provided the muscle needed to move massive pieces of furniture in and out of sets (and lived to tell the tale).

Suzanne Nelson, Managing Editor

Along with Lynette, Suzanne came up with the plan to create room settings in which to feature the quilts. Working to coordinate the selection of props, paints, furniture, and accessories, Suzanne was ever mindful of remaining true to the Thimbleberries look. This is the third time she has worked on a photo shoot with Lynette, so it is no surprise that her house is starting to look more and more "Thimbleberry-ish" every day.

Troy Schnyder, Production Assistant

No task was too small (or too large) for Troy to tackle with his characteristic grace. From carting huge pieces of oak flooring or 12-foot rolls of carpeting to arranging quick furniture deliveries, Troy knew how to make things happen.

Suzy Vesely, Stylist Assistant

The keeper of the prop room, Suzy faced the enormous task of keeping hundreds of props inventoried and shuttled back and forth between studios.

Furniture and Prop Credits

The following companies and businesses were extremely gracious in supplying furniture and photography props.

Antique Complex of Fleetwood
Route 222
Fleetwood, PA 19522
(610) 944-0707

Supplied decorative accessories.

Country Furniture, Inc.
Route 202 & Montgomery Avenue
Montgomeryville, PA 18936
(215) 362-3856

Supplied tables, chairs, beds, and other household furnishings and accessories handcrafted from the finest American pine.

The Country House
805 East Main Street
Salisbury, MD 21804
(800) 331-3602

The largest country store in the East. Supplied decorative accessories.

Forever Flowers
4266 Nazareth Pike
Bethlehem, PA 18017
(610) 861-5222

Provided fresh flower arrangements.

Fox Hollow Woodshop
4111 RD 4
Fleetwood, PA 19522
(610) 683-5150

Provided wooden toys.

Georgetown Manor
Ethan Allen Home Interiors
5064 Hamilton Boulevard
Allentown, PA 18106

Provided household furnishing and accessories.

Royal Furniture of Emmaus
637 Chestnut Street
Emmaus, PA 18049

Complete line of furniture and bedding from major manufacturers. Provided beds, chairs, and tables.

Sherwood's for Kids
20 South 3rd Street
Easton, PA 18042
(800) 982-KIDS

Supplied baby crib.

With Style Design Service
109 Wilden Drive North
Easton, PA 18045
(610) 253-5716

Supplied antiques and props.

I·N·D·E·X

211

METRIC EQUIVALENCY CHART
mm=millimeters   cm=centimeters

Yards to Meters

YARDS	METERS	YARDS	METERS	YARDS	METERS	YARDS	METERS	YARDS	METERS
$\frac{1}{8}$	0.11	$2\frac{1}{8}$	1.94	$4\frac{1}{8}$	3.77	$6\frac{1}{8}$	5.60	$8\frac{1}{8}$	7.43
$\frac{1}{4}$	0.23	$2\frac{1}{4}$	2.06	$4\frac{1}{4}$	3.89	$6\frac{1}{4}$	5.72	$8\frac{1}{4}$	7.54
$\frac{3}{8}$	0.34	$2\frac{3}{8}$	2.17	$4\frac{3}{8}$	4.00	$6\frac{3}{8}$	5.83	$8\frac{3}{8}$	7.66
$\frac{1}{2}$	0.46	$2\frac{1}{2}$	2.29	$4\frac{1}{2}$	4.11	$6\frac{1}{2}$	5.94	$8\frac{1}{2}$	7.77
$\frac{5}{8}$	0.57	$2\frac{5}{8}$	2.40	$4\frac{5}{8}$	4.23	$6\frac{5}{8}$	6.06	$8\frac{5}{8}$	7.89
$\frac{3}{4}$	0.69	$2\frac{3}{4}$	2.51	$4\frac{3}{4}$	4.34	$6\frac{3}{4}$	6.17	$8\frac{3}{4}$	8.00
$\frac{7}{8}$	0.80	$2\frac{7}{8}$	2.63	$4\frac{7}{8}$	4.46	$6\frac{7}{8}$	6.29	$8\frac{7}{8}$	8.12
1	0.91	3	2.74	5	4.57	7	6.40	9	8.23
$1\frac{1}{8}$	1.03	$3\frac{1}{8}$	2.86	$5\frac{1}{8}$	4.69	$7\frac{1}{8}$	6.52	$9\frac{1}{8}$	8.34
$1\frac{1}{4}$	1.14	$3\frac{1}{4}$	2.97	$5\frac{1}{4}$	4.80	$7\frac{1}{4}$	6.63	$9\frac{1}{4}$	8.46
$1\frac{3}{8}$	1.26	$3\frac{3}{8}$	3.09	$5\frac{3}{8}$	4.91	$7\frac{3}{8}$	6.74	$9\frac{3}{8}$	8.57
$1\frac{1}{2}$	1.37	$3\frac{1}{2}$	3.20	$5\frac{1}{2}$	5.03	$7\frac{1}{2}$	6.86	$9\frac{1}{2}$	8.69
$1\frac{5}{8}$	1.49	$3\frac{5}{8}$	3.31	$5\frac{5}{8}$	5.14	$7\frac{5}{8}$	6.97	$9\frac{5}{8}$	8.80
$1\frac{3}{4}$	1.60	$3\frac{3}{4}$	3.43	$5\frac{3}{4}$	5.26	$7\frac{3}{4}$	7.09	$9\frac{3}{4}$	8.921
$1\frac{7}{8}$	1.71	$3\frac{7}{8}$	3.54	$5\frac{7}{8}$	5.37	$7\frac{7}{8}$	7.20	$9\frac{7}{8}$	9.03
2	1.83	4	3.66	6	5.49	8	7.32	10	9.14

Inches to Millimeters and Centimeters

INCHES	MM	CM	INCHES	CM	INCHES	CM
$\frac{1}{8}$	3	0.3	9	22.9	30	76.2
$\frac{1}{4}$	6	0.6	10	25.4	31	78.7
$\frac{3}{8}$	10	1.0	11	27.9	32	81.3
$\frac{1}{2}$	13	1.3	12	30.5	33	83.8
$\frac{5}{8}$	16	1.6	13	33.0	34	86.4
$\frac{3}{4}$	19	1.9	14	35.6	35	88.9
$\frac{7}{8}$	22	2.2	15	38.1	36	91.4
1	25	2.5	16	40.6	37	94.0
$1\frac{1}{4}$	32	3.2	17	43.2	38	96.5
$1\frac{1}{2}$	38	3.8	18	45.7	39	99.1
$1\frac{3}{4}$	44	4.4	19	48.3	40	101.6
2	51	5.1	20	50.8	41	104.1
$2\frac{1}{2}$	64	6.4	21	53.3	42	106.7
3	76	7.6	22	55.9	43	109.2
$3\frac{1}{2}$	89	8.9	23	58.4	44	111.8
4	102	10.2	24	61.0	45	114.3
$4\frac{1}{2}$	114	11.4	25	63.5	46	116.8
5	127	12.7	26	66.0	47	119.4
6	152	15.2	27	68.6	48	121.9
7	178	17.8	28	71.1	49	124.5
8	203	20.3	29	73.7	50	127.0